Albert Ellis (Ph.D., Executive Director, Institute for Advanced Study in Rational Psychotherapy, author of *How to Live With — and Without — Anger*):

"A highly readable book, written in an exceptionally open style, that blends RET with some of the best elements of other schools of therapy. Will prove helpful to many people . . . "

Joel Fort (consultant, lecturer, author — The National Center for Solving Special Social Health Problems):

"Thank you for letting me go over your fine book, impressive for its openness and containing excellent exercises and valuable sayings."

Bill Glasser (author of *Reality Therapy, Positive Addiction*):

"This is the kind of book that most of us who practice psychotherapy would like to write and haven't yet been able to do. I am very much convinced that anyone who reads it will receive a great deal of help. It has a warm, personal and very therapeutic message."

Clark Moustakas (author of *Loneliness, Loneliness and Love, Creativity and Conformity, Finding Yourself, Finding Others*):

"I particularly was sparked with "Reborn," the opening chapter. The book as a whole offers me exciting moments and important resources."

John Powell (author of *Why Am I Afraid to Love?, Why Am I Afraid To Tell You Who I Am?, The Secret of Staying in Love*):

"I am personally grateful for the many insights I have derived from this book. After his many acknowledgments of all his gurus it will probably come as a surprise to Lee Silverstein that he has himself become a guru to many. I am sure that that will be the inevitable result of this book."

Sidney B. Simon (Ed.D., Prof. of Humanistic Education, University of Massachusetts):

"He takes paint, and canvas, and brush and pallet knife, and makes beauty. In this case, his paint was Reality Therapy, his canvas Rational Emotive Therapy, and his brush Values Clarification. With consummate skill, he has produced an incredible resource for practitioners in the helping professions."

Don't just hear words . . . pay attention to the feelings . . . "Please understand how I felt . . . accept my feeling the way I did . . . " Pause to ask, "What do you *really* want from me?" I don't want to listen to just what you say. I want to feel what you mean.

In order to see I have to be willing to be seen.

Silence
can mean:
Confidence, live and let live
— I am I, You are You —
affirmation that we are two people together,
that I accept you as one.

If a man takes off his sunglasses I can *hear* him better.

"Talking at" and "talking about"
are not communication.
Talking "at" vs. talking "with"
means we try to seduce
someone into thinking we are right
and also to sound right to ourselves.

Consider
the Alternative

by Lee M. Silverstein

With Jon Brett and Linda Roberts
foreword by Sidney B. Simon

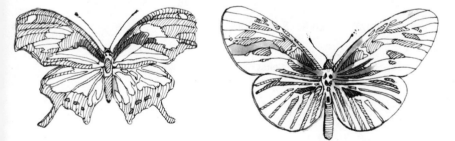

Published by

CompCare® publications

2415 Annapolis Lane, Suite 140, Minneapolis, Minnesota 55441
A division of Comprehensive Care Corporation

(Ask for our catalog, 800/328-3330, toll free outside Minnesota or 612/559-4800, Minnesota residents)

Dedicated to:

The thousands of Alcoholics Anonymous
members, who don't open the gates of Heaven
and let people in, but open the gates of hell and
let people out.
Who give alternatives when people see none,
Love when people feel they have none.
Who continue to do so . . . never judging
people, but helping them judge themselves.

Linda and Jon, without whose care, support
and encouragement, my own "vultures"
probably would have long since stopped this
project.

Doris, who lived so much of this, who is gone,
but will continue to be a part.

Thanks to:

Many thanks to those whose quotes, maxims
and snatches of songs have stayed with me over
the years. Though I have forgotten where most
of them came from, I like their warmth, wisdom
and humor and share them here for others to
enjoy.

Thanks to Archie Brodsky, whose caring
touches gave shape to the final manuscript.

To Diane DuCharme for her confidence in me
and Meredith Montgomery for her loving
preparation of the manuscript for the printer.

We can only
appreciate the
miracle of
of a sunrise

if we have
walked
in the darkness

For my gurus:

Leslie Jon Amy Barbara Phyllis Joan Sissy
Andrea Joe Frank Maureen Harry Liz George
Bill Kit Jeanne Clete Horace Danny Henri
Martin Albert Jerry Jack Tom Lois Al Virginia
Lenny Janice Janet Kris Monica Fitzy Eliot Bob
Sidney Linda Don Sheldon Archie Stanton Dory
Shel Hugh Jerome Sam Arthur Jonathan Jay
Jesus Jacques Nina Gabriel Sebastian Andrew
James John Cassian Pierre Luke Stephen Bruno
Billy Helen Raymond Zelda Pat Cal Rosewell
LeClaire Stanley Idres Charles Arthur Saul
Rebecca Clarke Rod Marcey Kathleen Victor
Margery Joel Eugene Eda Paul Carole Oz
Moses Natasha Morris Robert Smokey Judy
Jules Nancy Harvey Mary Alice Zerka Lud
Larry Max Ingmar Theodore Bunny Elaine
Mike Zorba Clare Pat Melanie Ken Agnes Milo
Herbert Joan Sally Preston Margaret Ernest
David MaryAnna Enes Peter Murray Ed
Eugene Betsy Gillian Pam Allen Erich Abraham
Fritz Carl Alan Lyn Ira Frances Rollo Carly
Marlo Mims Winnie Lucy Leon Ruth Wally
Sandy Andy Lorraine Antoine Edith Charlotte
Ivan Teo Susan Paul Bland Wil Anna Bertha
Willie Jesse Waylon Woody Vernon Betty
Lynda Cat Karen Ti Connie Anthony Ann
Eugene Roberta Sky Vinnie Audrey Terry Nikki
Exey Kevin MaryAnn Gus José Claire Roseanna
Hal Seb Chris.   Thanks, LMS

Acknowledgments

The author gratefully acknowledges
permission to reprint portions of:

Death of a Salesman by Arthur Miller.
   Permission given by author.

Equus by Peter Shaffer. 1975, Avon Books.
   Permission given by author.

Guru by Sheldon Kopp. 1976, Bantam Books,
   Inc. Permission given by author.

*If You Meet the Buddha on the Road, Kill Him:
   The Pilgrimage of Psychotherapy Patients* by
   Sheldon Kopp. 1972, Science and Behavior
   Books, Inc. Permission given by author.

Person to Person: The Problem of Being Human
   by Barry Stevens and Carl Rogers. 1967,
   Real People Press. Permission granted by
   Barry Stevens to quote a portion of her
   material.

Shoes of the Fisherman by Morris L. West.
   Permission granted by Wm. Morrow and
   Company.

The Velveteen Rabbit by Margery Williams.
   1958, Doubleday, Inc. Permission granted by
   publisher.

*The Wounded Healer: Ministry in
   Contemporary Society* by Fr. Henri J.
   Nouwen. 1972, Doubleday. Permission given
   by author.

Thanks also to the following for permission to
quote: Jenena Kurtz, Dr. Andrew Malcolm,
Theodore Rubin

the eye
with which
I see God
is the same eye
with which
God sees me.

Foreword

Lee Silverstein has written a book for an artist in humanistic psychology. Because he is an artist himself.

He takes paint, and canvas, and brush and pallet knife, and makes beauty. In this case, his paint was reality therapy, his canvas rational emotive therapy, and his brush values clarification. With consummate skill, he has produced an incredible resource for practitioners in the helping professions.

Lee is a weaver, too. He has woven a fabric of gentle simplicity. He has woven ideas into a framework that can be used. His inspiration and insights glisten like gossamer threads in this book.

Use it wisely, dear readers. He has given you tools and ideas and dreams. You will be better for having read this. Better in the ways that one feels in front of any work of art. Uplifted, hopeful, and clearer.

Sidney B. Simon, Ed.D.
Professor of Humanistic Education
University of Massachusetts
Author of:
> *Caring, Feeling, Touching*
> *Values Clarification: A*
>   *Handbook of Practical*
>   *Strategies for Teachers and*
>   *Students*
> *I am Loveable and Capable*
> *Meeting Yourself Halfway*

Contents

one   Reborn

two   Reeducation — Mine and Thine

three   The Desperate Ones

four   Involvement in Change

five   Small Changes

six   Breaking the Silence

Conclusion

Bibliography

I am a relationship ever-changing

one

Reborn

This book is a guide to self-development and a training manual in counseling for you who are learning to help and you who seek more effective ways of helping. It is also a personal testament. For me, these things fit together naturally. I was able to help others only after others had helped me. Whatever success I have enjoyed as a "helper" has come in great part from knowing what worked in my case — knowing how it felt to be given the support and guidance I needed to undertake the hard work of personal growth. Having gone through a life change myself, perhaps I can inspire you to change and to help others change.

Encouraged by friends and prodded by conscience, I write this book to share, as a professional, the methods that I have found successful in working with people who have difficulties in living. In describing my techniques, I also speak of the difficulties in living that I have had. I do so because I have found that Lee the therapist is at his best when he is simply Lee the human being. I do not believe in therapeutic distance, but in therapeutic *involvement* — a joining of hands in common humanity. When people come to me for help, I try to share their worlds as fully as I can and to share my world just as fully with them. Let me begin, then, by sharing a little of my world with you.

• • •

When I review the evolution of my life and the astonishing changes that have taken place in recent years, nothing should really surprise me. Up until ten years ago the world saw me as a successful Jewish salesman. But I never felt the success; I felt only the deep personal inadequacy I had felt all my life. So I deadened the pain with alcohol and drugs. Finally, because of some foolish, megalomaniacal business decisions brought on by the chemical distortions of my awareness, I found myself on the verge of bankruptcy — personal, spiritual, financial. There I was — a graduate of the illustrious Harvard Business School, a husband (albeit unfaithful, deceitful, detached), a father (albeit disinterested, neglectful, absent), a person, as John Lennon writes, "crippled inside" — wrecked with active alcoholism and drug-dependent, as I had been for twenty years, lonely, guilt-ridden, anxious about unknown fears, confused, alienated, suicidal (in practice as well as in thought) — a morally and spiritually bankrupt, live Peter Pan, seeking only pleasure, loving no one and committed to nothing. Paul Simon's song characterized me perfectly:

I've built walls
A fortress deep and mighty,
That none may penetrate.
I have no need of friendship; friendship causes pain.
It's laughter and it's loving I disdain.
I Am A Rock,
I am an island.

Irreverent, blasphemous, closed to all spiritual aspects of life, I came face to face with what proved to be a miracle. I am sure that many of you are as turned off by and skeptical of the concept of miracles as I was. But I am defining "miracle" in Webster's terms, as simply a "remarkable event." The remarkable event in this case was that I stopped drinking and taking other drugs. I became strong enough to accept the "pains" of living as experiences from which to learn rather than as problems to be avoided.

Since then, I have achieved reasonable happiness and comfortableness (certainly 100 percent more than I ever dared dream). I am entirely chemically free. I am willing to tolerate and live with feelings rather than seek their immediate reduction. I am learning that to fail is okay, to feel inadequate is okay, as long as I am willing to keep risking to rise again, to risk loving, to risk commitment, to risk involvement, to risk taking responsibility for myself. So what? You can hear thousands of "testimonials" like this at Alcoholics Anonymous, Overeaters Anonymous, Gamblers Anonymous, Recovery Inc., Synanon, Christian Science meetings, and churches. Perhaps in some sense my testimonial is no different from thousands of others, but my experience is unusual if not unique. I have successfully rechanneled the energy and intensity with which I led a deviant life, destructive to myself and to those around me, into a positive force, bringing love, nourishment, care and understanding to myself and others. I have converted the same marketing skills with which I so successfully sold material goods into an ability to influence change in people's lives, thereby bringing them greater satisfaction.

How did this miracle happen? It did not happen with the help of "analytic" psychiatrists who explored the deep-seated problems of my past. What good were their insights when they didn't give me any insights, and when they denied my present problem? One psychiatrist said, "No, alcohol isn't the problem. You can take a few drinks; just control it." Another refused to put me on Antabuse. And when I went to a rabbi and asked him whether I might be an alcoholic, he told me that "Jewish people don't have that problem." So much for insight therapy. So much for some of society's respected helping institutions. What did help was an association of people who had suffered just as I had.

My rebirth began with my entrance into Alcoholics Anonymous (AA). The laughter, the honesty, the fellowship that I sensed at my first meeting made me think, "Maybe these people have something." That first meeting made me feel comfortable in the same way my first drink had, only this wasn't an artificial chemical high that captured me even as it "set me free," but a truly liberating emotional high that gave me the strength to begin changing my life. In AA I became aware of the necessity of involvement with other people and the importance of sharing "experience, strength, and hope." For so many years I had felt pain alone and had chosen not to look at alternatives. But I learned that I could give

3

up alcohol and drugs with the help of others, in the caring, loving, nourishing environment that AA provided. This was the critical ingredient that had been missing in the past.

What happened next was like a series of heavenly visions one after another, only they were really earthly visions, so precious to me who had been denied them. I, who for more than five years had lived with daily thoughts of dying, of being released into death, was released into life. I, whose morning "exercise" for years had been retching (in AA we call it "making love to the toilet"), could step outside in the morning and breathe the air, see the sun, take in the world. I, who had known only the literature of pain and despair (I knew *Death of a Salesman* by heart), discovered the optimistic, loving spirit of Rod McKuen. I could not have been called culturally deprived, but when my wife took me to hear Beethoven (for her an unremarkable event), my reaction was, "Where has he been all my life?" That was my reaction to all these gifts of life and reality. I wondered why I hadn't known about these things, hadn't known of the world of love and beauty and shared feeling, hadn't known that I was not alone. So that I might further connect with that from which I had been estranged, I started to read all I could of Rod McKuen and libraries full of inspirational literature, and started to go to the orchestra and the ballet and collect classical music.

Next, I began reading about alcoholism, and soon I was taking some general courses on the subject offered by the Greater Hartford Council on Alcoholism. Turned on by a friend to the work of William Glasser — and later Albert Ellis and Sidney Simon — I thought, "Wow, this is just like AA!" For the first time I saw how many others felt the same loneliness, the same inadequacy I did, and how many concerned people there were trying to bridge the gap of human isolation. I wanted to be part of that concern and that effort. By the time I had been sober about six to nine months I was sufficiently interested in counseling to apply for a job at Blue Hills Hospital, which at that time did the most work in alcoholism of all the institutions in the area. Blue Hills was reluctant to hire me at first, but after three months of volunteer work I convinced them that I was serious enough to take on full-time responsibilities. Meanwhile, I took an introductory course in counseling and a course in group work at the University of Hartford. Introduced to Jerome Frank's *Persuasion and Healing,* I began going through bibliographies in psychology and other fields the same way I had devoured Rod McKuen. I would read anything, go anywhere, meet anyone, attend any seminar to get more tools, more understanding.

In order to obtain credentials in counseling, I took a master's degree at the University of Connecticut School of Social Work, since I would be able to get the M.S.W. in two years while still working full-time at Blue Hills. Majoring in group work, I did field placements working with so-called "burned-out" schizophrenics at a halfway house at the Northampton Veterans Administration Hospital and with children, adolescents, and parents at the Child Guidance Center in New Britain. The techniques of involvement I had learned while working with alcoholics at Blue Hills proved equally successful in these settings. While I was studying at UConn, outside seminars brought me into contact with Ellis, Glasser, and other leading therapists. I studied with Glasser in California and became his representative in the Connecticut area, as well as a Rational-Emotive Therapist under Ellis.

Once I had my degree I worked at Hartford Hospital as coordinator of the psychiatric day program, as director of social services, and finally as director of alcoholism services. During this period I began teaching group methods at the UConn School of Social Work, and Reality Therapy and other techniques at the Hartford Graduate Center and Eastern Connecticut State College. During this period, too, I began working with some dedicated associates, including Linda Roberts and Jon Brett, who have shared and participated in my search for new people, new material, new sources of knowledge and understanding. I have also stayed active in AA.

Naturally enough — and gratifyingly — my new awareness and responsibility have extended to my family life as well. While making some real, though ultimately unsuccessful efforts to save my marriage, I was also rediscovering (as one more essential corner of reality that was opening up to me) my children. When it came out that my youngest child had never seen me swim or play checkers, I realized how little of a father I had been, how little my children and I knew of each other. While the past cannot be made up, I resolved that the present and the future would be different. By now I think that I have become a pretty decent father, and that in spite of the divorce we have had a good family life, though from time to time the guilt, the feeling of being less than a capable father creeps in. (Ellis would say the guilt comes from damning myself for the feeling, not from the feeling itself.)

In writing this book, I feel as if I have been doing what is for me an unlikely thing in an unlikely place, for I wrote much of it in a Benedictine monastery high in the Adirondack Mountains. Having taken a sabbatical, I came to live temporarily with the brothers of Mt. Savior because after eight years of working as a "helper" I felt a need to reestablish my priorities and goals. As you probably can see in your own progress and in that of the people you are working with, change is not simple or total. It is a complex process, and a person may slip back at times. So it was with me. I had assumed such heavy teaching and administrative responsibilities in the field of addiction counseling that I found myself losing my primary dedication to the individual addicted person — and losing the basic satisfactions in my life and work that went with that dedication. Instead of working directly with people I was spending more and more of my time traveling, organizing, promoting. In other words, Lee the big shot was back in "business."

I came to Mt. Savior because I found my deeds different from my creeds, my practices different from my teachings. I was not dealing with my eating habits, my anger, or my lack of sleep. I came to try to learn how to balance work and leisure, to stop chasing compulsively after greater and greater achievements, to stop trying to live up to the tyranny of my own and others' expectations, to find serenity and peace in myself. I came to recover the simplicity and clarity of purpose that I had felt during my first months as a counselor, so that I could fully give to the individuals with whom and for whom I wished to work. And I came to write — to bring my reflections and experiences into focus for myself by sharing them with you.

I was settled at the monastery, learning the lessons of the monks and reading all the books that had sat on my shelf for so long. With sheer joy I was shoveling cow manure at 4:30 in the morning, and I was feeling better physically, mentally and spiritually than ever before. I had committed myself to working with the monks for a year or two. Then one night I received news that Doris, my ex-wife of twenty-three years, had an inoperable brain tumor. I don't know why Doris got sick. I don't know what power governs the universe. I only know that I found myself in a situation where I had to make certain choices. My decision was to leave the monastery, assume responsibility for my children, and provide what comfort I could for Doris. This I did freely, without guilt or remorse.

I left the beauty, the inner peace, and the solitude of the monastery only to find myself in one of the most stressful and painful situations I have ever endured. I have watched Doris die, witnessed the neglectfulness and incompetence of hospitals and insurance companies as well as the compassion of certain doctors and nurses, and suffered the agonies of my children's grief. I have experienced all the insecurities, and feelings of inadequacy, of being a single parent.

Yes, all these agonies crowded into a few months, and yet I have survived reasonably well. There is some paralysis from time to time, but I hear and listen to and act upon the lessons that I have learned so well from my teachers over the years and that I now pass on to my students. No one ever said, when I started to shape up, that it would be easy, and I do not tell anyone else that it will be easy. When I think of death as an alternative, or the living death I went through for twenty years, I will and do accept the NOW. I do, as Sid Simon says, the best I can. Thus, as I complete this book, I am standing face to face with an illustration of coping with pain that I dearly wish had not been given me. But when I consider the alternatives, I believe this is, in Harry Chapin's words, a "better place to be."

Professionally, too, I find myself in a "better place" as a result of my stay at the monastery and Doris's struggle and pain. I am directing the Human Services and Alcoholism Program at Rockville Hospital, where the more humane, flexible schedule I have set for myself lets me give all the people I see the attention they need without having to cut them off for lack of time. It is a pleasure not to be looking at my watch all the time, and I feel I'm really helping again.

● ● ●

By writing this book, I hope in some small measure to express my gratitude to those who have helped me — who have been my "GURUS," my teachers, my prides — and to offer some "light," some "hope," some "possibility" to those who now feel helpless, hopeless, powerless and to those who are trying to be "helpers." The way I do this in practice is through what I call a reeducation therapy process — a type of counseling whose primary tool is involvement rather than detachment. It is a type of counseling that concentrates on the here-and-now problems of a person's present behavior and feelings and offers practical alternatives for change. The chapters following will show you what this approach is all about: who the people who need help are, how they have been influenced by their social environment, and what approaches and techniques I have found most effective in helping them (individually and in groups) gain the confidence and ability to make positive choices for themselves. Each chapter concludes with some "value-clarification" exercises, as well as with some sayings I have gathered over the years (some are my own, some borrowed) which sum up the meaning of the chapter and can also be used as value-clarification material for groups.

For allowing me your hospitality and allowing yourselves the benefit of my experience — thank you.

What better than drugs?
Me.

You don't have to be a failure
to feel like a failure.

chapter one exercises

1. Stepping Stones
Take a few minutes to reflect on the nine most significant stepping stones which have brought you to this point in your life. Stepping stones are those main turning points or intersections, or as Dag Hammarskjold calls them, "markings" along life's path. They are not necessarily successful events, but may actually be failures of projects or efforts in which you have invested much time and energy. (Thanks to Ira Progoff.)

Do the stepping stones you choose surprise you?

Is the idea of a pathway not taken still there in your mind?

Can it be taken appropriately now?

2. Inventories
Make a list of:
   a. Twenty things you love to do.
   b. Twenty things you want to do before you die.
   c. Twenty changes you want to make in your life.

3. What I suggest now is that you take a sheet of paper and reflect on what you've read in this chapter and the insights you've gained from the exercises above by using Sid Simon's **Discovery Statements:**

I learned that _____

_____

_____

I relearned that _____

_____

_____

I was surprised that _____

_____

_____

I was delighted that _____

_____

_____

I was saddened that _____

_____

_____

I need to _____

_____

_____

What meaning do your "discoveries" have for you?

_____

_____

_____

_____

_____

_____

_____

_____

_____

_____

FIND YOURSELF
 KNOW YOURSELF
 BE YOURSELF

he who knows
   others is
   clever
he who knows
himself is
enlightened

two

Reeducation — Mine and Thine

The therapy I practice is based on what I learned (and continue to learn, for the process is never ending) in the course of my own reeducation. I needed many different guides to achieve a chemically free, reasonably comfortable existence, to help me keep my resolve, to control the impulses that want me to do differently when those "poor me's" take over, when I'm "down" because I'm not special or sensational enough. I look to the guides for support, for those "warm fuzzies" when I'm feeling "cold pricklies." And I'm ever so grateful that they are always there. These guides are my gurus.

What is a guru? A guru is a teacher — not a god but a guide. My gurus are those significant people in my life who have taught me how to become myself and feel comfortable with myself. Sheldon Kopp eloquently describes them as people who have achieved that very rare quality of being totally human. The guru is no magician, but merely a person "no longer expecting to be unafraid or certain or perfect. He gives himself over to being just as he is at the moment. He accepts fear, lives with his uncertainty, finds his imperfection sufficient."

I am a pupil to many teachers. My gurus include poets, songwriters, authors, entertainers, lovers, students, patients, fellow AA members, literary and theatrical characters, the monks of Mt. Savior, my family and my friends. I learn from everyone and everything I come in contact with, and my thirst for more remains unquenchable. I read anything I get my hands on that may give me additional insight into myself and the people I care for.

As I met my gurus, I was astonished to see that their

ideas and principles graphically illustrated the realities and experiences that I was painfully discovering in my own recovery. Over and over, I seemed to hear the same messages. The lyrics were different, but the music was the same. It turned out that my gurus have more in common than not, and that commonality represents the core of my own development and of what I teach to others.

The Gurus' Lessons

1. Take charge. First, I learned that I am in charge of my own being. All my behavior is the result of my choices. Even though my past may influence me, it is my choice to allow it to control my present. I drifted through much of my life without being aware that I had the potential to change — to do something differently. When I became aware of and accepted my choice-making power, I could then begin — if I chose, and I did — to direct my behavior toward a positive, more responsible way of life.

2. Act responsibly. In Bill Glasser's words, I can choose to "fulfill my needs in a way that does not deprive others of their ability to fulfill their needs. I accept the consequences of my chosen behavior. I have found that responsible behavior tends to create happiness, but unhappiness does not cause me to behave in an irresponsible way."

3. Focus on present behavior. It's important for me to focus on what I am doing "now," to look at what my present behavior is and how it might or might not be helping me. The "now" is important because I can't really change the past, but what I do "now" will influence the future. It's like the Sanskrit proverb, "Look to this day, for it is life," and the Carly Simon lyric, "Let's stay right here 'cuz these are the good old days."

4. Choose from alternatives a plan. In order to choose freely, I had better look at other ways of behaving — at alternatives. I must consider, evaluate, then decide on an alternative.

Choosing an alternative is the beginning. Then I must form a plan. My plan is my way of saying to myself that I want to start a new behavior, no matter how small, and begin to redirect my actions in a positive, more responsible manner.

5. "Do" the plan. Once I have made the plan I must "do" it. As AA taught me, "You walk the walk, not just talk the talk." Confession without change is a game.

The psychologist William James came up with three rules for starting any project. He said: 1. Do it immediately; 2. Do it flamboyantly, telling as many people as you can so you have a built-in support group to cheer you on and keep you from turning back; and 3. Don't make excuses or exceptions.

6. "Do" it over and over (and over and over). Any new behavior feels uncomfortable and painful initially. I must "do" it over and over until it becomes a way of life. Just as I learned the "bad," I can learn the "good" — by practicing it.

These are the principles which guide my life, which I teach to others, and which I recommend to you. Our goal is to reeducate people in the business of living, just as they educated themselves to act in self-defeating ways.

What This Approach To Therapy Is Not

Perhaps the best way to begin describing my approach to therapy is to list some of the ways in which it differs from many of the standard therapies, as well as from some common notions of what therapy is:

It has no orthodox methodology. Many "helpers" get so caught up in a methodology that they often forget their purpose. For them, the means to change take precedence over the needs of the person. There is no single, pure treatment modality which can be successfully applied to all people. The goal of discovering one is not realistic because every individual is unique.

My goal is to provide comprehensive treatment services for any persons who want them. I seek to design the services to be responsive to the needs of the people concerned, rather than to fit the people into established programs and methodologies. When appropriate, I often refer people to other "helpers" or sources of help to supplement the work I am doing with them.

It does not promise a total, permanent cure. No treatment program can guarantee a cure forever. People are dynamic, and relapses do occur. The initial change away from self-defeating behavior patterns represents only a beginning. Constant vigilance is needed to maintain the change. And change itself tends to be incremental rather than apocalyptic.

It does not rely on professional jargon or dehumanizing classifications. I do not use language that sets me apart from the person I am helping and separates that person from his feelings and experience. Rigid concepts and categories can make a person's difficulties seem more formidable than they have to be, both to client and counselor. In their place, I prefer to use whatever vocabulary helps the client understand his or her own situation in terms that are real to that person, and allows us both a fluid appreciation of his or her development.

It does not emphasize insight into the past and into sources of problems. Too much emphasis on the past can lock a person into a pessimistic, deterministic view of self and obscure the potential to choose a different course in the present. Insight is useful, but my first concern is with a more practical aim — to deal directly with the most serious problems a person has now, the ones that prevent him or her from functioning as a responsible, reasonably fulfilled person. Once that is accomplished, there tends to be an immediate, positive emotional change, a growth of self-esteem and contentment, such that insight into the past comes to be of secondary importance.

It does not have all the answers. The basic question I address as a therapist is, "How do we express in words and deeds our feelings over situations in which we find ourselves?" To be truly healthy human beings we must confront and accept our whole emotional repertoire. I attempt to aid the individual in the journey into self so that s/he may get in touch with and hopefully own those feelings that lie deep inside. (By "own" I mean make them his or her own, understand them, be comfortable with them, live by them without being ruled by them.) In the end, however, we can depend on no one but ourselves in

alcoholism
comes both
in people
and bottles

I never felt I measured up
because I was using the wrong yardstick —
I measured myself against someone else
instead of myself.

We constantly rotate between
"For my sake the world was created"
and "I am dust and ashes."

Confession is often an avoidance of change . . .
"I confess. It's beyond my control."

the investigation into our feelings. Ultimately, we are left alone to ponder our gut reactions to issues.

As a "helper" I don't claim to have all the answers. I'm reminded of Sheldon Kopp's book, *When You Meet the Buddha on the Road — Kill Him.* I cannot be a Buddha for another, for the true Buddha can only be found within oneself. I am but a guide along the road of life to help people find the meaning inside themselves — to explore without terror. I help them look inside until they tap the resources of their Buddha.

What This Approach To Therapy Is

Often it is easier to say what something is not than what it is. I cannot provide rules or set patterns to describe what I do when I do "my thing" with people, nor can I supply an analysis of how and why it works. Someone once asked my dear friend Marilyn, "How does Alcoholics Anonymous work?" With beautiful simplicity she answered, "Just fine, just fine." In my counseling practice I've been lucky. More people than not (a "reasonable" guideline again) have achieved a reasonable degree of comfort after they have had discomfort and a reasonable degree of happiness after they have been unhappy. Most important, they have achieved hope after long periods of hopelessness. How have I helped accomplish this? My methodology is eclectic and flexible. It is a design that lacks design, one that is situational and dependent on what is happening "now" between human beings.

A cafeteria of gurus. With regard to its theoretical grounding, I like to think of my treatment program as a "cafeteria of gurus." The cafeteria includes, but is not limited to:

Human potential movement	Erhard Seminar Training
Creativity training	(EST)
Bioenergetics	Gestalt training
Humanistic education	Rolfing
Psychosynthesis	Reality Therapy
Effective education	Arica
Silva Mind Control	Values Clarification
Awareness training	Rational-Emotive Therapy

Transcendental Meditation (TM)	Transactional Analysis (TA)
	Primal therapy
Sensitivity training	Assertiveness Training

Out of all these sources, I would say that three are central to my approach. Basically, I superimpose the concepts of Values Clarification, as outlined by Sidney Simon and his associates, on William Glasser's Reality Therapy and Albert Ellis's Rational-Emotive Therapy. Throughout this book you will find illustrations of how you can employ these three theoretical frameworks and the others I have listed to help people want to help themselves.

Theory and practice. No theory of human growth will do any good unless it is put into practice through an authentic personal relationship. I try to establish that relationship by being the same person I am anywhere else, with an added dimension of professional consciousness. The "techniques of involvement" that I will describe in Chapter Four are expressions of my personal background and my experience as a counselor — what I am, what I have observed, what I have accomplished.

Having worked in the trade union movement and sold insurance to all kinds of people, I find it easy to be comfortable with people and make them comfortable with me — to accept and be accepted on many levels. As they say in AA, you don't "compare," you "identify." My experience is not "comparable" to that of homeless alcoholics living in a Salvation Army Center, but there is much in their experience as alcoholics — and as human beings — with which I can identify, and vice versa. They feel anxious; I feel anxious. They feel lonely; I feel lonely. They feel inadequate; I feel inadequate. We all can identify. You will not be exactly like me, but you will undoubtedly have skills that complement mine. Your personal style will be different from mine, but you can be the kind of caring person who makes a difference in someone else's life.

When people come to me who are having difficulty in living, basically what I say to them is, "Come dine with me. Talk with me. Let me care. Let's get acquainted and look at the problem together. Let's look at what you've been doing. Are you happy with it? Is it helping you? Let me share with you what has worked for me and/or for others. Let me show you what some of the gurus have had some luck with. I won't give up on you even if you give up on yourself. Let me reach out and let's walk together." That is my commitment — not to give up on a person. I say, "You've been tending to yourself for a long time. Now we're going to tend together, that is, explore, care and *learn*. First you'll learn by working with me, then with others, then with your world. This time you can learn to do it in a better, more successful way."

In subsequent chapters we will see how these guiding principles and sentiments work out in practice, in specific situations in individual and group counseling. But first let's ask ourselves a couple of questions: Who are the people we're trying to help, and how did they get to be the way they are?

Accept what is . . .
accept reality as reality is NOW.

To not be aware is nowhere.

chapter two exercises

1. Gurus
Make a list of your gurus. Keep in mind that gurus can include family, friends, lovers, authors, composers, poets, singers, teachers, students, entertainers, and literary and theatrical characters.

2. Admirable People
Make a list of ten people whom you admire and respect and in each case note one primary reason why you feel as you do.

How do the qualities you respect in others "mirror" those you want to be associated with yourself? What's missing? What do you want to begin to do differently?

3. Before we go on to the next chapter, let's redo the **Discovery Statements:**

I learned that _____

_____

_____

I relearned that _____

_____

_____

I was surprised that _____

_____

_____

I was delighted that _____

_____

_____

I was saddened that _____

_____

_____

I need to _____

_____

_____

What meaning do your "discoveries" have for you?

_____

_____

_____

_____

_____

_____

_____

_____

_____

_____

_____

_____

_____

_____

Because we are afraid to love

I am alone.

three

The Desperate Ones

Just like the tiptoe moth
They dance before the flame
They've burned their hearts so much
That death is just a name . . .
They watch their dreams go down
Behind the setting sun . . .
And underneath the bridge
The waters sweet and deep
There is the journey's end
The land of endless sleep
They cry to us for help
We think it's all in fun
They cry without a sound
The desperate ones.

What kind of person was I eight years ago? Who are the people I deal with today? Who are all the "desperate ones" of whom Jacques Brel sings?

They are the victims of the "American Ego" Erich Fromm spoke of when he depicted the boredom, the loneliness, the anxiety that plague modern man. These are the people seeking courage and love, and relief from fear, rejection, and inadequacies. These are the people who more or less successfully keep the secret of their loneliness. These are the people who are afraid to try the unfamiliar, the unknown, afraid of "newness," afraid of the burden of "freedom." Aren't we all? As Kris Kristofferson sings:

Voices behind me still bitterly damn me
For seeking salvation. They don't understand.
Lord help me to shoulder the Burden of Freedom
And give me the courage to be what I can.

Cries From the Heart

The pain of isolation, uncertainty, and fear is most eloquently expressed in great literature and art. This is how Ishmael begins the story of *Moby Dick:*

> Whenever I find myself growing grim about the mouth;
> whenever it is a damp, drizzly November in my soul;
> whenever I find myself involuntarily pausing before coffin
> warehouses, and bringing up the rear of every funeral I
> meet; and especially whenever my hypos get such an
> upper hand of me, that it requires a strong moral
> principle to prevent me from deliberately stepping into the
> street, and methodically knocking people's hats off —
> then, I account it high time to get to sea as soon as I can.
> This is my substitute for pistol and ball. With a
> philosophical flourish Cato throws himself upon his
> sword; I quietly take to the ship. There is nothing
> surprising in this. If they but knew it, almost all men in
> their degree, some time or other, cherish very nearly the
> same feelings towards the ocean with me.

Job, the Biblical character, also longs for death as a release from suffering:

> Why is light given to him that is in misery,
>   and life to the bitter in soul,
> who long for death, but it comes not,
>   and dig for it more than for hid treasures;
> who rejoice exceedingly,
>   and are glad, when they find the grave?
> Why is light given to man whose way is hid,
>   whom God has hedged in?
> For my sighings come as my bread,
>   and my groanings are poured out like water
> For the thing that I fear comes upon me,
>   and what I dread befalls me.
> I am not at ease, nor am I quiet;
>   I have no rest; but trouble comes.

These are universal experiences. But there is a special kind of suffering — the kind which stems from anxiety, estrangement, drift, ennui — that characterizes modern life. Contemporary art gives voice to this pain, and the voices that we hear are our own. Neil Sedaka expresses well the feeling of alienation:

There was a man
A lonely man
Who lost his love
Through his indifference
A heart that cared
That went unshared
Until it died within his silence.

Dory Previn captures the terrible pain of loneliness:

would you care to stay till sunrise
it's completely your decision
it's just the night cuts through me like a knife
would you care to stay awhile and save my life?

John Lennon dramatizes the anguish of isolation:

We're afraid to be alone,
Everybody's got to have a home.
Isolation!
The world is just a little town.
Everybody trying to put us down.
Isolation!

The sense of lonely desperation and drifting without meaning is conveyed by Roberta Flack when she speaks of people "passing through the night and missing all the stars" and by Harry Chapin as he looks for a "Better Place to Be":

If you want me to go with you
It's alright with me,
Cause I know I'm going nowhere
And anywhere's a better place to be.

These are the people for whom real death is not the worst thing — only the last.

How is this pain expressed in life? It is manifested in tantrums, delinquency, crime, sociopathic and psychopathic behavior. It is expressed emotionally in depression, anxiety, phobias, and hysteria. It is seen in "craziness" or psychotic acts. It is experienced as psychosomatic illnesses, like headaches, neckaches, backaches, sinus trouble, migraines, hypertension, heart disease, asthma, allergies, duodenal ulcers, ileitis, colitis, chronic diarrhea, urinary urgency, and arthritis. Or, as was my experience, it may be deadened by substitute satisfactions such as alcohol, drugs, food, work, gambling, sex (remember the hero in the film *Carnal Knowledge?*). It is most traumatically expressed as complete withdrawal by those who commit suicide. We don't have to worry about *them* anymore, right?

The Desperate Society

We cannot talk of the "desperate ones" without considering the influence of the cultural environment in which they live — in which *we* live. Our culture loads us down with inhuman, impossible expectations. It does so because it knows that we listen to these — we would make them up ourselves without the cultural training. We teach ourselves to be the "best" or the "most," to be "good" or "sweet" all the time, to evaluate ourselves as failures or successes. We teach ourselves to seek instant gratification of our needs and wants, rather than to work toward a long-term solution. And when we don't achieve the success, live up to the ideal, attain the gratification, we learn to reduce our feelings — to neutralize them, get rid of them — rather than to tolerate them and accept the pain of dealing with them. (Society *does* teach us to reduce certain feelings like murderous anger. We overlap and learn to reduce many other feelings as well — feelings which might do us some good if we let ourselves experience them.) Out of this contradictory, destructive ethos come drug use and other expressions of escapism and despair.

As we grow up, we receive mixed messages which create conflict within us as to what kind of person we really are, as Barry Stevens relates in *Person to Person*. She cites such examples as:

> Sit nicely. Leave the room to blow your nose. Don't do that, that's silly. Why, the poor child doesn't even know how to pick a bone! Flush the toilet at night because if you don't it makes it harder to clean. DON'T FLUSH THE TOILET AT NIGHT — you wake people up! Always be nice to people. Even if you don't like them, you mustn't hurt their feelings. Be frank and honest. If you don't tell people what you think of them, that's cowardly. Butter

knives. It is important to use butter knives. Butter knives? What foolishness! Speak nicely. Sissy! Kipling is wonderful! Ugh! Kipling (turning away).

The most important thing is to have a career. The most important thing is to get married. The hell with everyone. Be nice to everyone. The most important thing is sex. The most important thing is to have money in the bank. The most important thing is to have everyone like you. The most important thing is to dress well. The most important thing is to be sophisticated and say what you don't mean and don't let anyone know what you feel. The most important thing is to be ahead of everyone else. The most important thing is a black seal coat and china and silver. The most important thing is to be clean. The most important thing is to always pay your debts. The most important thing is not to be taken in by anyone else. The most important thing is to love your parents. The most important thing is to work. The most important thing is to be independent. The most important thing is to speak correct English. The most important thing is to be dutiful to your husband. The most important thing is to see that your children behave well. The most important thing is to go to the right plays and read the right books. The most important thing is to do what others say. And others say all these things.

All the time, *I* is saying, live with life. That is what is important.

But when I lives with life, other I says no, that's bad. All the different other I's say this. It's dangerous. It isn't practical. You'll come to a bad end. Of course . . . everyone felt that way once, the way you do, but *you'll learn!*

Such conflicts too often are not dealt with, but are swept out of sight. Yet all those suppressed doubts, longings, sufferings that our culture prefers not to acknowledge are still there, clamoring to be put to rest by the next drink or the next fix.

Our culture is a conspiracy against time and tension. Reduce the time like a Polaroid camera, from a moment to an instant, the sooner the better. TV dinners, chord organs, microwave ovens, speed reading. Reduce the tension by living "better" through chemistry. Take care of "bad" feelings, psychic pain, with an "Rx"tra. Society, conspiring with the benign physicians (who with all due

Yale or jail,
Park Avenue
or park bench...

they're all the same
to drunks.

Loneliness
is the
major disease
of our era

respect have neither the time nor the training to deal with these aspects of a person's life), gives us permission to escape. We have a new population of "Libriolics" and "Valiolics."

Our broadcast and advertising media are continually creating a new demand for drugs. There are drugs for "illnesses" such as sleepless nights, tiredness, anxiety from traffic jams, nervous tension, irritability and fatigue — drugs that are a "cure-all" for the tensions and problems of everyday life. The technologists and pharmacologists, professional pushers, keep supplying us with more and more advanced instant gratifiers and instant "successes." We solve our problems with "magic pills." My guru Arthur Miller states:

> The problem is not to undo suffering . . . or to wipe it off the earth . . . it should inform us . . . so we regard it as a necessary part of existence and try to pluck from it what growth and wisdom we can, instead of trying to cure ourselves of it constantly, and to avoid it, and to avoid tension, avoid conflicts, and arrive at a lobotomized sense of what they call happiness in which nobody learns anything, but an ultimate informed indifference . . .

Joel Fort wisely warned us years ago of the price we would pay as "Pleasure Seekers." We learn drug behavior. It is reinforced and perpetuated by our culture, and behavior that is reinforced is repeated.

Dr. Andrew Malcolm, a Canadian physician, has coined the term "chemophilic society" to connote the present era:

> A chemophilic society is one in which an abundance of intoxicating drugs is available to a large number of people who are receptive to their easy use. We live in such a society today, even though our full potential for drug dependence has certainly not yet been realized. We are progressing constantly, however, and some day, if we can only remain as calm and sophisticated as we now seem content to be, we will discover that the process has become irreversible.

Heroin and alcohol are the fastest panaceas of the chemophilic society. The search is always on for automatic comfort.

Society creates the very deviant subculture that it works to undo. The irony of "rehabilitation programs" is that we teach people to delay gratification and to tolerate feelings, and then we demand that they live in a world that encourages the opposite behavior. The truly magnificent Jon Weinberg says that the recovering alcoholic must strive for "superior, not just average, emotional adjustment because in our society the average person at times uses alcohol and other drugs instead of internal coping mechanisms. This is a luxury the sober alcoholic cannot afford." We are presented with a set of value contradictions. We live in an environment that promotes instant gratification and feeling reduction, thus perpetuating the behaviors that can ultimately lead to an addiction (drinking, drugs, gambling, work, sex). Yet while society approves of and indeed encourages moderate drinking, moderate gambling (lottery, horserac-ing, cards), the Protestant ethic of work, and some kinds of sex, it doesn't approve of the addiction to these things. It is a crazy-making process.

An additional irony is that while our culture cultivates immediate gratification, it continually tells us to wait. Wait for grade school, wait for high school, wait for college, wait for a job, wait for a promotion, wait for retirement, wait for death, wait for "Godot." Some find that you really don't have to wait. You can "get off" here. "Get it while you can," as Janis Joplin used to cry. And she "got off" the merry-go-round early. While we're waiting we can take the "help" (alcohol, drugs, gambling, etc.) that society offers. The dilemma is: "NOW — BUT WAIT; NOW — BUT WAIT."

The main question is one of lifestyle — how to live in this society, and with what values. These are questions that get us closer to our "mission" (if you'll pardon that terrible word) — helping people who are battling between hope and despair, fear and courage, love and hate, between the animal and the angel. It's the good old "human predicament." The solution lies not in letting our pharmacology catch up or waiting for our machines to do electro-shock better, but in risking involvement with people.

Sanity, Madness, and Social Control

How does a society which routinely submerges trouble-some feelings in the interest of convenience treat people who have emotional difficulties? Not by risking involvement with them and encouraging them to risk involvement with their own emotions. Instead, as we have already noted in the case of doctors who rely on the dispensing of tranquilizers, expediency is the rule in dealing with disruptive emotional conflicts and even with simple deviance. People who violate society's definitions of sanity are diagnosed into ready-made categories. The category determines the treatment, without regard to the uniqueness of the person. A perfect example of unwarranted labeling and destructive judgment is found in Sheldon Kopp's book, *If You Meet the Buddha on the Road, Kill Him.* It is the tragically true story of a mistaken admission to a state mental hospital:

> I once witnessed an ironically enlightening instance of the cultural definition of insanity, and of the power politics of psychiatric social control. At the time when I was on the staff of a New Jersey State Mental Hospital, a strange man appeared on a street corner in Trenton, wearing a long white sheet and quietly muttering 'gibberish.' His very presence threatened the certitude of sanity of the community at large. Fortunately, for the sheeted man's own good, a policeman was called by some saner citizen. So it was that this poor man was able to be brought under the protective lock-and-key of his local Asylum.

> His efforts to explain his strange behavior were offered in vain, since it was clear that he was a looney, or to be more scientific, he was diagnosed into that catch-all garbage can of a syndrome known as Schizophrenia, Chronic Undifferentiated Type. It would have been difficult for anyone to acquit himself well in that diagnostic staff situation, since the patient was assumed to be crazy until proven sane, unrepresented by counsel, and not even told that anything he said could be used against him.

> One further limitation was in play, accruing epiphenomenally from the sociology of American medicine. Foreign-trained physicians are not allowed to practice medicine in this country until they have demonstrated competence both in English and in medicine. So far, so good. However, in the absence of such

proven competence, they are permitted to work as resident psychiatrists in state mental institutions. I have seen irascible (but otherwise normal) citizens diagnosed as confused psychotics, adjudged incompetent, and denied their civil rights and their freedom on the basis of their inability to understand the incompetent mouthings of ill-trained resident psychiatrists whose own command of English was so limited that I could not understand them either.

Fortunately for the white-sheeted, gibberish-muttering patient in question, the hospital Visitor's Day began the very next morning. Evidently he had called home and made his plight known. That morning twenty other people wearing white sheets arrived at the hospital. Equally strangely clad, they were also equivalently incomprehensible to the psychiatric staff. It turned out (to the resident psychiatrist's amusement) that these men and women were all members of the same small rural church sect, a religious group who defined their identity in part by clothing themselves in the purity of white cloth, and by being divinely inspired to talk in tongues. The psychiatrist in this case, being a practicing Roman Catholic (who weekly ate and drank the body and the blood of Jesus Christ) thought they were a queer bunch indeed. Heaven help him should he ever wander into a community in which his own religious affiliations would be equally obscure. The patient was released that afternoon. One such man is a lunatic. Twenty constitute an acceptable and sane community.

The same critique of psychiatric diagnosis and treatment is made eloquently in Peter Shaffer's play *Equus*. In this story a psychiatrist is faced with "curing" a young boy deemed "insane" by his social environment. In the following passage, Dr. Dysart reflects on the fact that in "curing" the boy he will destroy a very important, creative aspect of the boy's personality. What constitutes a "cure"?

I'll heal the rash on his body. I'll erase the welts cut into his mind by flying manes. When that's done, I'll set him on a nice mini-scooter and send him puttering off into the Normal world where animals are treated *properly*: made extinct, or put into servitude, or tethered all their lives in dim light, just to feed it! I'll give him the good Normal world where we're tethered beside them — blinking our nights away in a nonstop drench of cathode-ray over our

Immediate gratifications
are seldom immediate solutions.

When I examine my fantasies
for the values they express
I am surprised at the pettiness.

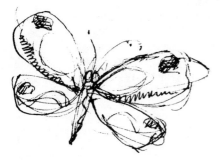

Insecurity can mean lack of self-knowledge:
I am not secure with myself —
I can't rely on myself.
I am not secure with myself —
I don't know how I operate.

*Or insecurity can mean I know how
I operate but don't think it is good enough.*

shrivelling heads! I'll take away his Field of Ha Ha, and give him Normal places for his ecstasy — multi-lane highways driven through the guts of cities, extinguishing Place altogether, *even the idea of Place!* He'll trot on his metal pony tamely through the concrete evening — and one thing I promise you: He will never touch hide again! With any luck his private parts will come to feel as plastic to him as the products of the factory to which he will almost certainly be sent. Who knows? He may even come to find sex funny. Smirky funny. Bit of grunt funny. Trampled and furtive and entirely in control. Hopefully, he'll feel nothing at his fork but Approved Flesh. *I doubt, however, with much passion!* . . . Passion, you see, can be destroyed by a doctor. It cannot be created.

As Kopp concludes,

> . . . the protective efforts of the self-appointed 'sane' influence the whole field of psychiatry and psychology. The clinical diagnosis of psychopathology is too often a form of social control. If other people make us nervous by the foreignness of their queer talk and odd behavior we give *them* tranquilizing drugs or lock *them* away in custodial institutions.

The very same issues arise in Ken Kesey's *One Flew Over the Cuckoo's Nest,* the story of a present-day mental institution in Eugene, Oregon. Like Peter Shaffer and others, Ken Kesey challenges the notion of the sane community versus the insane community as he leads the reader through the metamorphosis of McMurphy, a rough and tumble, highly energetic ex-con. By the end of the novel McMurphy has been reduced to a lobotomized idiot. The use of electric shock is but one example of impersonal treatments that don't constitute a cure, but merely serve as a form of social control. As Theodore Rubin says, "Treating a depressed person with electric shock is like hitting a fine but broken Swiss watch with a hammer. If it starts to work, we fool ourselves into believing that the trouble is over — for a while." Is this how we deal with those whose greatest crime was perhaps nothing more than the attempt to be themselves? Is it necessary to hinder, cramp, and murder the creative forces of a human being who doesn't totally conform to social norms? My notion of cure (and I don't believe in the word) would be not to restrict the individual, but to lead him to the freedom which would allow him to become aware of himself and aware of the choices he is faced with in living with other human beings in a social environment. Those choices imply responsibility. It is responsibility I wish to cultivate. There are, however, many steps to this process, and the entire process, like anything else worth doing, takes time.

The first step is involvement. The people who come to me (like myself, in my hopeless days) have often been dealt with reprovingly by family, pleadingly by friends, brutally by jails, cynically by doctors, sentimentally by the clergy, and scornfully by the social workers. Whatever "name" they go under, the "helpers," protectors, partners, enablers have often missed the critical issues of involvement and caring (other than "Cheer Up" or "Shape Up" or "We all got problems" or "I felt sorry 'cuz I had no shoes until ... " etc.). Involvement is more than cheerleading, more than consolation. It is an active continuing process. It is the essence of the helping relationship, the *sine qua non* of counseling.

chapter three exercises

1. Identifications

What personal meanings do the quotes in the text have for you?

Think of the times in your life when you've had problems so bad you'd rather die than face them.

What do you consider your "Burdens of Freedom"?

Think of the times in your life when you've felt lonely either when alone or in a crowd of people.

What are your greatest fears?

Think of a time when you were faced with two opposite demands at the same time.

2. Again, the **Discovery Statements:**

I learned that _____

_____

_____

I relearned that _____

_____

_____

I was surprised that _____

_____

_____

I was delighted that _____

_____

_____

I was saddened that _____

_____

_____

I need to _____

_____

_____

What meaning do your "discoveries" have for you?

_____

_____

_____

_____

_____

_____

_____

_____

_____

_____

_____

_____

_____

_____

IF WE'RE LONELY IT'S
BECAUSE WE BUILD WALLS

INSTEAD OF BRIDGES.

four

Involvement in Change

Influenced by my sabbatical at the monastery, I can't help but think of personal regeneration in spiritual terms. Consider the parallel to the religious tenets of sin and repentance. Sin, in its truest sense, means "missing the mark." To return to the "mark" we have to repent. We must clear our conscience and forgive ourselves for our "sins." We must not continue to condemn ourselves as "bad" or "evil," but rather set a new "mark" and start on a new path. This is our "resurrection" — our rebirth. In the way that some plants, as they die each year, throw off seeds of new life, we can renew ourselves. Instead of a human "being," let each of us be a human "becoming."

The question is, "How to return to the 'mark'?" What is the answer to the modern predicament? For some, it is the "Now" of Zen, For some, it is Fritz Perls saying, "Don't push the river; let it flow by itself." Maybe we push the river too much in our constant search for the "instant high."

For some, it is the monastic way of life. The monks seem to be comfortable within themselves when nothing is happening. They are able to be silent without getting uptight or embarrassed when they have nothing to say, without thinking, "I have to say something, impress someone, fill in the silence." They have a feeling of belonging to themselves and not to the world. They feel a part of themselves, not apart from themselves.

For some, it is AA and other such groups. Within the fellowship and love of AA, the "fractured," the mutually vulnerable, the walking wounded can hold each other and provide mutual support.

But what of Joe or Jane Average who wants to deal with a personal problem? He or she does not have the benefit of involvement in a group like AA. Aren't we all Joe or Jane Average looking for and hoping for "Resurrection," change, the possibility of a new life? Fritz Perls once stated, "To suffer one's own death and be reborn is not easy." No, it's not easy, but consider the alternative.

What we are looking for is a renaissance (a rebirth of learning), a "reeducation," an ability to step back and look at the "wreckage" with someone we trust, who we feel really cares, who will encourage us to have the courage and the power to let go of the familiar — to risk. We seek the openness to look at what is going on in order to change. What makes possible that openness to change is *involvement* — the creation of an atmosphere of warmth, caring, nourishment, understanding, and trust. Involvement is the same thing whether it takes place in a monastery, an AA chapter, a therapy group, a one-to-one counseling relationship, or a friendship.

The creation of a caring, loving atmosphere to facilitate change is a major theme in the work of Sid Simon, the humanistic educator whose concepts I believe will be the cornerstone of rebuilding trust and communication in our society. Many of my "gurus" speak on the very same subject, only using different words:

AA calls it "fellowship."

Glasser calls it "involvement."

Gordon calls it "acceptance."

Rogers calls it "unconditional positive regard."

Jesus calls it "brotherly love."

The Old Testament says, "Love thy neighbor as thyself."

Buber calls it "I-thou."

Jourard calls it "invitation to being."

Clark Moustakas, John Powell, and countless others have their own names for it.

Involvement as "Hospitality"

What is involvement? It is, first, a recognition of everyone's unique individuality *and* common humanity.

In a beautiful sermon at Mt. Savior Monastery, Father James Kelly, taking as his text "Thou Shalt Not Kill," expanded it to: Thou shalt not kill another person's spirit, kill by not appreciating another's uniqueness, kill by some nonverbal look, kill the integrity of another, eliminate, judge and lose sight of another's individuality. At the monastery, the day ends with compline services. In the darkness, all the monks appear the same, yet each one is special in his own way. One's a great mechanic, one specializes in horticulture, one's a terrific cook. They're all different, yet they're all the same.

Dory Previn sings in "The Midget's Lament" of the midget who is looked at with the attitude that "if you've seen one midget, you've seen them all." The midget has "half the heart, twice the pain; half the heart, twice the pain." Our stereotypes block our involvement with people and blind our vision to their similarities and differences. Who was "sweet Marilyn Monroe on the silver screen" or "sweet beautiful Jesus on a painted cross?" Dory Previn wants to know their "person" — did Marilyn ever have a headache; did her mama own a gramophone? Was Jesus jealous of his father; did he like to walk on water?

Despite all our differences, we still share, as human beings, many of the same feelings. A quotation that I would like to see on every "helper's" desk, with a copy given to every person they work with, is this one from Sheldon Kopp's Guru:

My pain hurts as yours does. Each of us has the same amount to lose — all we have. My tears are as bitter, my scars as permanent. My loneliness is an aching in my chest, much like yours. Who are you to feel that your losses mean more than mine. What arrogance! . . . I feel angry at your ignoring my feelings. I live in the same imperfect world in which you struggle, a world in which, like you, I must make do with less than I would wish for myself . . . And too, you seem to feel that you should be able to succeed without failure, to love without loss, to reach out without risk of disappointment, never to appear vulnerable or even foolish . . . Why? While the rest of us must sometimes fall, be hurt, feel inadequate, but rise again and go on. Why do you feel that you alone should be spared all this? How did you become so special? In what way have you been chosen? . . . You say you've had a bad time of it, an unhappy childhood? Me too. You say that you didn't get all you needed and wanted, weren't always understood or cared for? Welcome to the club!

Let's meet people as they are, and not with prerequisites. Let's meet people where they are, and not where we'd like them to be. According to my friend Henri Nouwen, a priest who is currently on the faculty of the Yale Divinity School, if we are *all* compassionate, we can understand and share suffering, we can each be the support for the other, we can feel the pain by joining, listening, learning, and showing strength together.

Father Nouwen believes that alienation and hostility represent the prevailing attitude of our culture. We are all strangers to one another, and a new relationship almost always commences with suspicion, discomfort, and distrust. To overcome this pervading sense of alienation and hostility, Father Nouwen has devised the concept of "hospitality" as a prior condition for true involvement. Hospitality is simply an offer to a stranger of breathing room or free space. "Hospitality, therefore, means primarily the creation of a free space where the stranger can enter and become a friend instead of an enemy. Hospitality is not to change people, but to offer them space where change can take place." When Henri discusses hospitality, he does so not only in terms of outright stranger relationships, but also in terms of personal relationships that are often entangled with egos and expectations: parent-child, teacher-student, healer-patient.

Hospitality comes through the richness of "poverty." It is manifested in the poverty of mind, a mind that has learned to unlearn unnecessary rationale and intellectualizing so that pure contact can be made. It is manifested in the poverty of the heart, a heart that has given up prejudices, worries, jealousies, and all that is implied in egoistic possessiveness. True hospitality is not colored by selfish motivation. According to Henri, "Once we have given up our desires to be fully fulfilled, we can offer emptiness to others. Once we become poor, we can

"You're wrong"
means
"I don't understand you . . .
I'm not seeing what you're seeing."
But
there is nothing wrong with you;
you are simply not me,
and that's not wrong.

be a good host. It is, indeed, the paradox of hospitality that poverty makes a good host. Poverty is the inner disposition that allows us to take away our defenses and convert our enemies into friends." I bow to the extreme "poverty" of the monks at Mt. Savior Monastery.

Therapy as Involvement

Establishing a therapeutic relationship means creating an alliance of equals. That is the first step, but it is also a continuing step, because if you lose the involvement you lose the opportunity to help. I build involvement by listening accurately and speaking relevantly, so as to establish and maintain a communication that is genuine on both sides and genuinely shared.

The first step is a welcoming — an atmosphere that says, as Helen Sorenson, my dear, late friend of the Salvation Army used to say, "Hello there, you are welcome here." Wow, what a meaningful experience to someone who for so long has felt that he's had no one. As Linda, in Arthur Miller's *Death of a Salesman*, says to Biff and Happy during Willy Loman's most depressed and oppressed days, "But he's a human being, and a terrible thing has happened to him. So attention must be paid." Attention had better be paid to a person as a unique, totally "human" being.

I try to come to a person empty, void, with poverty of mind, devoid of assumptions. Upon meeting new people I try to avoid making judgments. I try to avoid unpardonable statements such as "Oh, oh, I had one like him last year." Instead, I say, "Come on, find yourself, know yourself, be yourself. You no longer have to be anyone else." When I got to AA, it was the first time I didn't have to be my father's son. I didn't have to be like my brother-in-law or like anyone but Lee. They gave me "permission" to be me, and for the first time I felt that I belonged. "That's how I'll be with you," I promise. "I'm not going to teach you what to do, but I'll sure help you learn how to do it." As Rod McKuen put it:

I know no answers
To help you on your way
The answers lie somewhere

At the bottom of the day.
But if you've a need for love
I'll give you all I own,
It might help you down the road
Till you find your own.

That is the "hospitality" of the therapist. You are there not to do it yourself, not to give out the answers, but to make a space in which others can know themselves.

One way I help people know themselves is by letting them know me. I keep in my mind the picture of the self-disclosing, caring "helper" that the late Sidney Jourard, a Third Force Power, evoked in his writings. Disclosure begets disclosure. I can best elicit sharing in others if I share of myself. Not only will I care, but I will listen to you accurately, I will speak relevantly, I will share and give what I can of me and my experience, I will share my "wounds," as Father Nouwen says in *The Wounded Healer*. According to Nouwen, the counselor must not only listen to the other person, but must also possess the qualities of personal concern, faith in the value and meaning of life, and hope. He must be in touch with his personal and professional loneliness and thus be able to create an atmosphere of hospitality and community. In a word, the "helper" must be willing to take personal risks to facilitate a close involvement. "No one can help anyone without becoming involved, without entering with his whole person into the painful situation, without risk of becoming hurt, wounded, or even destroyed in the process." That's why I share my feelings, attitudes, opinions, experiences, my history and my relationships with others where that information is relevant. I will care as much as I can and share as much as I can. In our sharing relationship, both of us are permitted to be authentically ourselves.

Facilitating Change

As a "helper" I work toward the goal of getting people to believe that they can change, that they can gain the confidence and the power, and indeed have had within them all along the power to change. "You have the power, the choice to do differently, and I'll work with you so you can be free." In *The Wizard of Oz*, when the scarecrow asked for brains, the wizard replied, "You don't need them ... Experience is the only thing that brings knowledge, and the longer you are on earth, the more experience you will have." When the lion asked for courage, the wizard replied, "You have plenty of courage, I am sure ... All you need is confidence in yourself." The false wizard was, after all, a true wizard because he realized that the cure for our weaknesses and maladies comes not from a "magic" source, but from tapping the inner power of our selves. The cure lies in getting down to the Buddha that lies within.

Just as the wizard could provide no "magic" cure, neither can a "helper." Only action on *my* part can change my behavior. In *Shrinks, Etc.* Thomas Kiernan comments that psychotherapy can offer comfort, but that it does not cure psychic disorders. He warns against having false expectations and delusions about psychotherapy itself. In fact, he says, perhaps all one can expect from psychotherapy is to gain some new insight about oneself through introspection.

What is the change that the Buddha within can make, and that we can help along? I think of it as the change from being "fractured" to being "open."

"Fractured" persons are the casualties of the chemophilic society. They are the people who are beset by anxiety; who lack an identity that allows them to take hold of themselves, to take charge of their health and their educational and emotional development. They are uninvolved and feel inadequate to cope with other people and with their environment. They are constantly seeking immediate relief from outside sources, blaming other people, places and things for their problems, rationalizing their behavior, and suffering remorse and guilt about their thoughts and actions. They have a pervading sense of loneliness and resent what others "have." They suffer from "psychosomatic" illnesses and ailments, are dissatisfied with home and job, and constantly seek quick solutions such as a "geographical cure" ("If I move from here, that will be the answer"); a job change ("It's the boss"); a change of spouse ("No one could put up with him/her"). They experience unknown fears and anguish and are preoccupied, even obsessed, with protecting their self-destructive behavior. The feelings of the "fractured" person are best summed up by Neil Sedaka when he sings, "Just waking up brings you down."

Some people, especially those seeking help, reach a "bottom" point, at which all or some of the pain comes together to force them to look at what is going on and what they can or cannot control. Then they start the journey toward becoming an "open" person. This change of attitude, this new belief, this admission of their true state of being, coupled with an acceptance of where they want to go and the possibility of getting there, provides an openness to CHANGE (not just to adjustment). This is what I strive for with the people with whom I work.

As people climb the ladder of "openness" they begin to put themselves together physically with good eating, working, and sleeping habits. They become believers in practicing and accepting the consequences of their behavior, in staying in the "here and now," in setting some "rights" and "wrongs" for themselves, and in distinguishing between their "needs" and their "wants." They stop making excuses for their behavior. They may achieve some sense of "spiritual" value. They thrill as they begin to become involved with people and their environment, and as the tension, the fear, the anxiety and the loneliness give way to reasonable happiness and comfort.

Stages of growth. In my own experience and in my work as a "helper" I have found that individuals go through three stages in the process of changing their lives and reeducating themselves.

First, they "won't" do any differently from what they are doing. They are "happy"; they "eat, drink and are merry." Then they go through a stage where they feel they "can't" do any differently. No way out. No exit. No alternative. "I can't" is an improvement over "I won't" because it represents a breaking down of defenses, an admission that change would be desirable. Usually, in fact, "I can't" *means* "I won't." When I begin to work with people, they tend to be in one of these two stages.

ideas
are
straight...
but

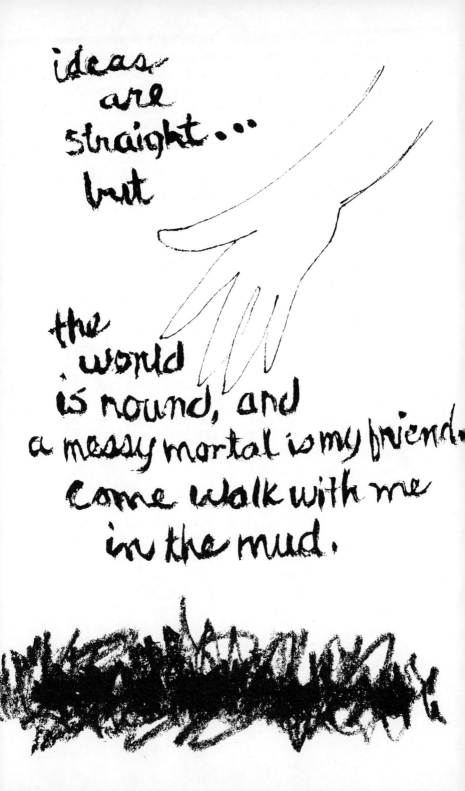

the
world
is round, and
a messy mortal is my friend.
Come walk with me
in the mud.

Finally, there is the stage that actually makes my eyes teary and puts a lump in my throat. It's that stage where they say, "Maybe I can." "Maybe I can do differently." That stage is what Jerome Frank refers to so eloquently in his concept of Hope. The goal of a "helper" is to get people to this stage. Because I lived as a "fractured" person for so long I can still taste the thrill, the "high" I felt when I discovered that "Maybe I can change," that "Maybe I have the ability to make another choice" — to choose a different way. I reexperience this discovery with others who reach this stage of openness to change.

How People Change

In my work with people I have learned that certain attitudes and approaches on the part of a "helper" can be very helpful, while others usually are not helpful. How do people change? Not by being criticized. The last thing people need when they lack self-confidence and a sense of wholeness is to be driven to doubt themselves even more. That's why I have worked to get almost all the negative commentary out of my therapeutic procedure. Rather, I like to say that "people learn and change by being listened to, touched, validated, supported, and offered alternatives." These are five important ways in which a "helper's" involvement is expressed. Let's look at each one:

Listening. Listening means actively listening. Many of us hear, but few of us listen. Instead we are caught up in the age-old primal cry: "How may I ever be emancipated?" And the Zen Master's answer: "Who has ever put you in bondage?" "I'm stuck" is the cry. And we cry and we cry and we cry. We have got to learn to listen. This point is comically highlighted in the following Zen story told by Sheldon Kopp:

> Starting out as he does in the urgency of his mission, it is difficult for the pilgrim to learn this patient yielding. This is to be seen in the old Zen story of the three young pupils whose Master instructs them that they must spend a time in complete silence if they are to be enlightened.
> 'Remember, not a word from any of you,' he admonishes. Immediately, the first pupil says, 'I shall not speak at all.'

'How stupid you are,' says the second. 'Why did you talk?'
'I am the only one who has not spoken,' concludes the
third pupil.

As Paul Simon stated in "The Boxer," "A man hears
what he wants to hear and disregards the rest." We must
learn to listen if we are to help find alternatives. Sid
Simon's exercises stress eye contact, full attention,
noninterruption, and all things essential for opening our
ears to someone else.

We must hear all that is being said — we must, in fact,
go beyond mere words and truly listen to the other
person. Listening encompasses attending to the total
person — to the tone, inflections, and modulation of his
voice, to his facial expressions, his gestures, his body
posture, and other nuances of communication.

Touching. The touching I am talking about is not sex (as
I will make clear toward the end of this chapter). Nor is it
encounter-group touching. It is the simple physical
touching that expresses friendship and affection, and it is
also a touching of the spirit. What touches the spirit is the
quality of our involvement. I will do whatever I have to do
to engage with a person and to get that person to engage
with me. Some people (for example, alcoholics referred to
me by doctors) come to me involuntarily and at first reject
me. I come back to them again and again with the same
friendly greeting until my commitment gets through to
them. That's what I mean by touching the spirit.

Validating. Validation (positive acceptance) by a
therapist helps encourage self-validation (self-accept-
ance). When I start seeing someone, I say, in effect, "You
can't be ugly to me because I, like the Velveteen Rabbit,
understand." *The Velveteen Rabbit,* a selection from
children's literature, illustrates beautifully the concept of
being "real," of being unconditionally accepted.

As "helpers" we have to help find unique answers for
unique people. They have to discover or rediscover their
own uniqueness. They have to love themselves so that
they can get involved with other unique people and a
unique world. They have to find the "best" and look with
what Art LeBlanc calls "positive eyeballs," or they will

stay locked into the "worst" and continue to be blinded by their negative eyeballs. If they persist in saying, "I have nothing; I am nothing; I have nothing I can do; there is No-Thingness in me," they will always see the "awfulness" that Albert Ellis speaks of in their situation and in the people around them.

We should all practice looking at the world with "positive eyeballs." Sid Simon's exercise in self-appreciation and the idea of a National Validation Day reinforce this concept. Where do we learn to validate others? Where do we practice? We can begin with ourselves, then progress to the people with whom we live. For example, we could thank our spouse for a good meal or our child for some small job he or she did. There is no end to the truly deserved positive feedback that we can give.

Supporting. Support is expressed by our initial commitment: "I won't give up on you." It is expressed all along the way by the specific positive feedback we give whenever someone makes a small advance, and by our reaffirmation of commitment whenever someone falls back.

What AA said to me was, "If you'll stop, we'll try to help you find love, worth, and happiness. If you'll deal with your pain, through our love, fellowship, care, concern, involvement, we'll help you get along." They said that once I decided *what* I wanted to do or was willing to do, they'd back me all the way.

What I now say to others is, "I know that up until now you have been afraid, you have feared rejection, but I want to help and I know you have the power. If you, together with me, will look at worlds other than the one you have been in, you just might do better." As Carole King wrote and sang, isn't it good to know "You Got a Friend"? We can't do it alone. We've tried "our" way and failed. We all need a guide to aid us on the road to ourselves. I've yet to see any data that shows any form of therapy better than a simple helping relationship.

Offering alternatives. Just deciding to change behavior is only the beginning, in the sense that we then have to look at and evaluate new possibilities. Being told in my active alcohol days that my problem was alcohol didn't

namaste

sanskrit word meaning
" I salute that
in you
which is divine."

Being an alcohol counselor
is like being a whore;
everyone wants to know
how you got into the business.

The only difference between a drunk
and an alcoholic is that the drunk
doesn't have to go to all those meetings.

Breaking anonymity is like losing virginity.
Once it happens to you,
you wonder why you protected it so much.

really help me stop drinking, since I saw alcohol as not only the problem, but also the solution (if you'll pardon the pun). What choice was I given? Give up booze? For what? To get pain and misery? I couldn't stop hurting by just stopping drinking. Being told to stop was like being given ice in the winter.

A person's acceptance of responsibility for his own life and evaluation of his present behavior do not directly lead to behavioral change. They can simply lead to an acceptance of the problem. As Bill Glasser has stated so often, "Live it or give it up." As "helpers" we can try to help people find new meaning in their lives, to replace their paralysis with ACTION. Victor Frankl says that the enemy of boredom is "meaning" and that we have to find that meaning in the NOW. What we can do is to help people use their minds and imaginations to taste the freedom, to stand up to themselves and others, to be free to respond to the world . . . that's RESPONSIBILITY. We can lead people to affirm, to prize, to shout their aliveness, to open awareness and to make them care what happens, to get them excited about real possibilities. We can help them look for beauty in the world, for joy, for newness, and we can help them open creative channels. The limits of our ability to help are only as great as the limits of our imagination to suggest other possibilities for people.

Some Thoughts on Involvement

Just in case some of my enthusiastic passages on involvement seem to strike a note of starry-eyed idealism, let me bring them down to earth with some reflections based on my professional experience. In the next chapter I'll get into the specifics of carrying out the principles of involvement — how you validate, how you support, how you offer alternatives, and so forth. But before moving on to those week-by-week matters, I want to share with you some cautions and some practical suggestions concerning the general question of involvement.

Involvement is effort — loving effort — and imagination. Involvement can't be restricted to a fifty-minute hour. For me, it goes on all the time. It means constantly looking at the world for what it can mean to someone else. Whatever I do or see, I try to think, "How would this help or interest someone I care for?" Thus I find myself always cutting things out of newspapers and magazines, writing notes, making phone calls, recommending books and films and records. Sometimes I keep up with people by means of occasional cards and phone calls long after they terminate our formal relationship, especially in cases where they remain stuck in the "I can't" stage.

Even the normal requirements of the job, if you take them as seriously as I do, call for a lot of extra thought and effort. Involvement means being on time for appointments and to make or receive calls. It means calling people when you are concerned about them, and calling and calling until you reach them. It means being hospitable to calls at any time of day or night, within reason. It means persevering with unreceptive clients. It means devising unique methods for dealing with every individual and every group. It means coming prepared with books or records that are appropriate for a given individual or group at a given time. It means making notes about people and reviewing them so as to have the relevant information available whenever it may be needed. It's a lot of work. And I love every minute of it.

Involvement is serious — and funny. If I sometimes make counseling seem a forbiddingly heavy job, I should add that I have found humor a great tool both for establishing and maintaining rapport and for keeping my own balance. I know what anguish is, what rejection is. I grew up in a house of anger; I grew up a Jewish boy in a Yankee town; I grew up with facial paralysis. As a boy I cultivated a sense of humor as a defense against those sorrows, and I've been using and enjoying it ever since. You often can get through to people — get some truth through to them — with a joke. When you get people laughing, at least for that moment they won't be depressed. Humor also has a destructive potential, and my background has sensitized me to that, too. I stay away from that kind of humor, and I use humor at all only in the context of a trusting relationship where my intent will be

By leaning on someone you love,
you help to hold him up.

**The criticism that hurts the most
is the one that echoes
my own self-condemnation.**

"You ought to" really means "I want you to."

The problem is not "will power;"
it is "won't power."

Do I avoid looking a stranger in the eyes
because I don't want to make him uncomfortable,
or do I turn my eyes so he can't look into me?

understood. Poking fun at the ludicrousness of a person's behavior is fine as long as it is done in a spirit of fun and a spirit of love.

Involvement has its limits. At the same time as I approach my clients as friends (and many of them become my friends), I need to maintain a certain professional objectivity, both for their sake and mine. I call that being "involved, but not entangled." When I say, "I care as much as I can," I am referring to the fact that people sometimes want me to be other than what I am — to be a lover, a parent, whatever. If I were to try to be any of those things, I would lose the poverty of emotion that makes me a good "helper," and I would be risking destructive consequences for my own life.

The most serious violation of the ethics of involvement, and perhaps the most common, is, of course, sexual relations with clients. This issue is likely to come up even if you don't want it to; a woman once threatened suicide if I didn't have an affair with her. I have been attracted to some women I have worked with, but I won't bite. I won't even date someone who used to be a client, for when can you say that the counseling relationship has stopped?

Where a human life and human emotions are on the line, it is cruel to exploit your own power and another person's vulnerability. If someone claims that sex is just one more "technique of involvement," I reply that I'll believe him (it's usually "him") when I see him apply that technique with young and old, attractive and unattractive, male and female alike. This is an area where there is no leeway. If you justify it once, you can justify it again. I can't ever justify it, and I won't work with therapists who don't observe the same guidelines.

Involvement is more than a one-on-one thing. In keeping with my "cafeteria" concept, it's a good idea to be familiar with all the local therapists and community resources that can be of use to the people you work with. Some of the groups and agencies to which I refer people are Alcoholics Anonymous, Overeaters Anonymous, Weight Watchers, mental health clinics, consciousness-raising groups, self-improvement courses, dance lessons, and arts and crafts centers. I usually make these referrals to supplement my own work with clients, but I also make them in cases where I don't work well with someone, where my methods simply don't accomplish much, and I feel that the relationship should not be continued.

Many therapists, when a counseling relationship proves ineffective, go on seeing the client instead of referring him or her elsewhere. In those cases it's usually ego or money that keeps the therapist from doing what is best for the client. When you're not doing much good for someone, or when someone can't easily afford your services, it's better to send that person to a free clinic or an inexpensive group, or suggest a book to read. For example, someone who has a problem of dependency in love relationships may get as much from reading Stanton Peele's and Archie Brodsky's *Love and Addiction* as from a series of therapy sessions.

Another important resource to bring to bear, whenever possible, is the family. You cannot hope to deal with problems affecting family life and relationships — for example, alcoholism, "the family disease" — without involving the family. Otherwise you may deal successfully with one symptom of a family's conflict, such as drinking, only to find other disruptive problems still present. Involving the family also can enable you to verify or discredit information you get from the person you are working with.

Since you won't always get the full cooperation of the family, you have to do the best you can. Sometimes you can work with a husband and wife together; sometimes you have to work with them separately. Even if a couple or a family will not meet together on a regular basis, try to get at least one meeting with that "ogre" you've been hearing about from your client. It's good to have a real image of a significant person in the client's emotional life, to have seen and heard the nuances of the person's voice, appearance, and manner, rather than to rely on a phantom image based on distorted descriptions.

Involvement doesn't always mean confidentiality. I have an understanding with the people I work with that confidentiality will be maintained except in some fairly unusual cases where it would be destructive to do so. I do not want to help people be irresponsible or perpetuate their problems, and so I do not feel bound to confidentiality where it would only let them harm others or evade themselves. For example, a husband told me about an affair he was having but said he did not want it brought up in sessions with his wife. With his wife unable to interpret what was going on because she lacked an essential piece of information, the meetings became a meaningless charade, and I stopped seeing that couple.

● ● ●

Morris L. West says in *The Shoes of the Fisherman:*

> "It costs so much to be a full human being that there are very few who have the enlightenment or the courage to pay the price . . . One has to abandon altogether the search for security and reach out to the risk of living with both arms . . . one has to embrace the world like a lover . . . one has to accept pain as a condition of existence . . . one has to court doubt and darkness as the cost of knowing . . . one needs a will stubborn in conflict, but apt always to total acceptance of every consequence of living and dying . . . "

I agree; I had to learn these lessons for myself. Someone once said, "The bird needs a nest; the spider, a web; man, friendship." Warmth and caring and involvement. That's a big part of the answer. The rest of the answer is in the steps by which we guide someone to discover and embrace alternatives.

chapter four exercises

1. Positive Eyeballs

Make a list of the people who turn you off.

Have you really taken the time and tried to discover the uniquenesses in these people that you can learn to love and care for?

Make a contract with yourself to spend some time with these people to discover their uniquenesses.

2. Validations

Think over the last 24 hours. Who did something for you, or what small change did you notice about a person's appearance or behavior, that you did not take time to acknowledge because it seemed too small, too silly, too inappropriate, too out of line? (With appreciation to Art LeBlanc for the above two exercises.)

Send five validating notes positively reinforcing some "goody" you saw someone do for himself or herself, for you, or for other people.

3. Guess what? That's right. Let's do the **Discovery Statements** again.

I learned that _____

_____

_____

I relearned that _____

_____

_____

I was surprised that _____

_____

_____

I was delighted that _____

_____

_____

I was saddened that _____

_____

_____

I need to _____

_____

_____

What meaning do your "discoveries" have for you?

_____

_____

_____

_____

_____

_____

_____

_____

_____

_____

_____

_____

_____

A plan is only
my decision to imagine
a different future,
and if followed too rigidly
it precludes
spontaneous happenings.

five

Small Changes

Now that we have some sense of our general goals as "helpers" and of the kind of nourishing atmosphere that supports those aims, what can we do specifically to bring about personal change, whether in ourselves or in others? What are the attitudes and actions of a person who is making the commitment to growth and change, and how can a "helper" encourage those attitudes and actions? What, in outline, is our program of personal development, our program of therapy?

The Here and Now

The first thing we have to do to facilitate change is to place ourselves squarely in the "here and now." Past history is usually bad history, and we don't need to reinforce that. We are going to work beginning today. What is going on now? What are you doing now? What would you like to do now? We are *not* victims of past traumas. We must abandon seeking reasons for why things took place and focus on what is and what could be. As Robert Kennedy, quoting George Bernard Shaw, so eloquently stated, "Many men look at things as they are and say, 'Why?' I dream of things that could be and say, 'Why not?' " My gurus are very existential. They and I use the past only when we can focus on some past good or successful behavior.

I focus on behavior, not feelings, because I know that when I started changing my behavior, my feelings started changing. If I'm doing something OK, I'm likely to feel OK. "I understand how you feel, but what are you going to do?" is a familiar question in my repertoire of responses.

This is not to deny the value of insight, but only to affirm the fullness of the present as a source of insight and as the field on which the struggle for change is fought out. The "here and now" orientation is particularly important when we deal with people (for example, drug and alcohol abusers) for whom the changing of self-defeating behavior is the primary and immediate purpose of therapy. The suicidal person with whom we establish a strong involvement just to keep her alive long enough to begin working on her problems, the child molester for whom we recommend aversion therapy just to keep him out of jail, the alcoholic struggling to keep his life as well as his liver from disintegrating — for these people, time is of the greatest importance, and the time is NOW.

In focusing on "here and now" behavior, we must not lose sight of the fact that all of us bring to our present remnants of our past, particularly those reinforcements from others which have contributed to defining our sense of self. All of us carry self-condemning beliefs in our own inadequacies. Sid Simon calls these beliefs "vultures." "Vultures" are those self-put downs that are learned through the critical remarks "awarded" to us by other people as we grow up. (Of course, we would probably award ourselves self-criticism even if others did not teach us to do this.) Vultures are all those ideas of badness and inadequacy that crop up in the areas of intellect, sex, physical appearance, family relations, social skills and relationships, and creativity. A school-related "vulture" is well conveyed in Albert Cullum's vignette of a student's words to this teacher:

I was good at everything
— honest, everything! —
until I started being here with you.
I was good at laughing,
playing dead,
being king!
Yeah, I was good at everything!
But now I'm only good at everything
on Saturdays and Sundays . . .

"Vultures" can really get to us and give us such fear that we refuse to act. We get stuck because the "vulture"

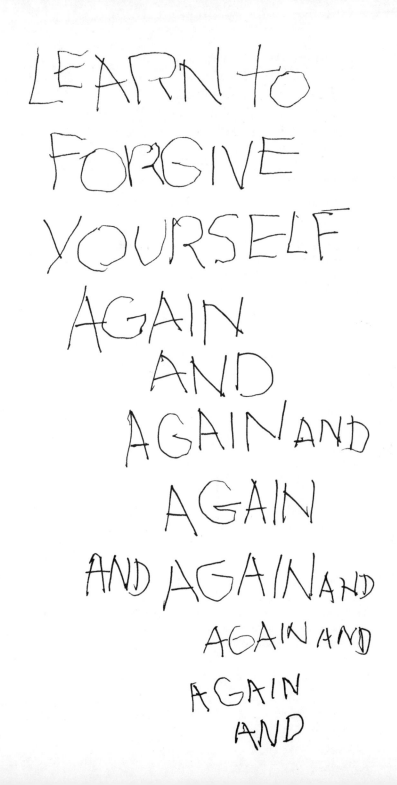

Sometimes the only way for me to
find out what it is I want,
is to go ahead and do something.
Then, the moment I start to act,
my feelings become clear.

**Being myself requires taking risks with myself,
taking risks on new behavior,
trying new ways of "being myself,"
so that I can see how it is I want to be.**

I don't feel "I want."
I feel "I lack."
I decide "I want."

I am more careful now when I make the jump from "I feel" to "I want."
I see now that this jump is the difference between feeling a lack
and deciding best how to fill it.

attacks and claws at us for so long that we accept this brutal attack as a natural phenomenon. *A Chorus Line*, a hit musical show, should have a subtitle, *A Line of Vultures*. The show contains songs such as "Tits and Ass" which tell of the supposed physical inadequacies of a young woman looking for work in a Broadway show. She seeks plastic surgery which alters her physical appearance, but her negative perceptions — her "vultures" — about her body remain.

I often think of my "vultures" and their destructiveness; that I have no mechanical ability, that I am "klutzy" in new social situations, that I'm not as attractive as others, that others are more gentle, more intelligent, more contemplative than I, that they are "real" and I am not. The "Junior Prom material" keeps coming back. The pain of Janis Ian's "At Seventeen" is relived at ages 27, 37, 47, and so on.

> To those of us who knew the pain
> of valentines that never came
> and those whose names were never called
> when choosing sides for basketball
> It was long ago and far away
> The world was younger than today
> and dreams were all they gave for free
> to ugly duckling girls like me

As Theodore Rubin points out, "How easily we say, 'I hate this or that about myself,' without awareness of the depleting effect that follows." We must face our "vultures" and forgive ourselves for our own inadequacies. "Lord have mercy. Christ have mercy. Let me have mercy on me."

Friend and guru Jenena Kurtz has made some keen observations on the subject of "vultures":
1. Vultures want only the dead and passed away. We should live in the present in order to keep them away.

Memories are really what make the vultures so horrible. If we did not remember how bad we were or how bad someone said we were before, then we would make no bad assumptions about ourselves. (Ellis would say the opposite: if we did not make and invent and asininely continue bad assumptions about ourselves, then we wouldn't remember how bad somebody said we were. Either viewpoint is okay.) How can something jab us mercilessly when we refuse to recall it?

Good memories can be vultures, too, when we dwell on them and long for the same things to happen again just as they did before. We can recall these happy events provided we enjoy them for what they were and as pleasant thoughts in the present. We can use them for the present *and* the future so long as we recall those responses that were successful, those that we can and want to use again.

To recall the bad response or outcome is only to reinforce a failure, which leads some people to believe that they are total failures in an area or, worse, total failures as people.

This is a good principle to practice when helping with another person's discipline, too. One can stop dragging up the past and pecking away at the person. One's efforts can be concentrated on dealing with the present and guiding the person to successful responses.

2. Another thing vultures do is sneak up on us. Some unfortunate people have subtle vultures — they may continually hang onto the negative and ignore the positive aspects of themselves until they get to the point where they are unaware of what they are doing and, therefore, become convinced that the negative is all there is.

3. Vultures appear to be fierce, strong birds, but "despite their formidable appearance they are weak, timid birds, whose only defense is to vomit decayed meat on a molester." In a sense we do this when we bring up to consciousness the old, decayed memories of how bad we are. The molesters are none other than ourselves. And how we are overcome by the formidable appearance of our faults! In actuality we are being overwhelmed by our own weaknesses. To recall the good about ourselves will make us strong; to recall the bad will only make us weak.

We should build up our own personal reserves by storing up and incorporating all the good qualities we see in ourselves. Also, by living in the present, we can fortify ourselves against the illnesses caused by bombarding our consciousness with harmful memories of the past. Then, if the vultures come, they won't seem so horrible to us. Most of them will go away if they have nothing to feed on.

Responsibility

In reviewing my own experience, I found that it was only when I stopped looking outside myself for excuses for my behavior, for the "if only's," the "should's," and the "poor me's," that I reached the stage of "Maybe I can." I had to admit that I was totally responsible for my own behavior and to accept the frightening realization that I, and only I, could change. I really do control my life! When I speak at an AA meeting I say, "My name is Lee, and I'm an alcoholic." I'm saying that whether an active or inactive alcoholic, I'm prepared to accept the natural consequences. No one controls whether I drink or not, except me. I am responsible. Pretty heavy, huh?

What we are looking for at this stage is surrender, a giving up of defenses, and an acceptance — without self-pity — of what we need to do. It is looking at all the rationalization and the blaming — "it's the hostile environment" — "it's my parents" — "it's the job" — all the excuses we don't think we're guilty of. It is eliminating all the denial that has dammed up our sense of responsibility for the consequences of our lives, and accepting the natural consequences of our behavior, good or bad.

Unwillingness to assume responsibility for oneself is expressed in "if only" statements. I used to say to myself, "If only I wasn't born with facial paralysis." "If only I wasn't born Jewish." "If only — if only — if only." If we continue to give in to these old beliefs instead of beginning to believe we are in control, we will not be able to cross the hurdle and overcome our self-defeating behavior. We are always rationalizing, blaming, procrastinating, avoiding the need for change. "Don't wait for the Day of Judgment; each day is a Day of Judgment," Camus said.

The tendency to place blame outside ourselves is satirized in this poem by Ann Russell, the comedienne:

I went to my psychiatrist to be psychoanalyzed
to find out why I killed the cat and blacked my husband's eyes,
He laid me on a downy couch to see what he could find,
And here is what he dredged up from my subconscious mind:
When I was one, my mommie hid my dolly in a trunk,
And so it follows naturally that I am always drunk.
When I was two, I saw my father kiss the maid one day,
And that is why I suffer now from Kleptomania.
At three, I had the feeling of ambivalence toward my brothers,
And so it follows naturally I poison all my lovers.
But I am happy; Now I've learned the lesson this has taught;
That everything I do that's wrong is someone else's fault.

It's too easy to place the responsibility elsewhere. The "traditionalists" in therapy see us as "victims." Are we "victims" or do we play at being "victims"? As guru Don Pet always says, "It's not always a fair world." The idea is to "be a just man (person) in an unjust world" (Camus). To do this, we must accept responsibility, accept the fact that we are in charge of our own lives. In the words of the AA Serenity Prayer, we must have the ability to accept the things that we cannot change, the courage to change the things that we can and the wisdom to know the difference.

I heard a story recently that is reminiscent of my own past denial thinking. A man noticed that he got drunk when he drank Scotch and water, bourbon and water, rye and water, gin and water. Noticing the problems that resulted, he decided that his problems had a common element. So he gave up water. This story is not so far-fetched. Irrational and unreal beliefs usually stem from some small part of a real situation. We have to cut through the rationalizations and focus on the reality. Only when we get at the reality can we look at what, if anything, we choose to do.

Here we get into the evaluation of our behavior. It is in this area that my friend Albert Ellis shines. He is one of the true giants of psychotherapy, for he has taught us all to question, to challenge, and to contradict all that irrational behavior and those "crazy" ideas we've had

HEALTHY
ANGER—

when I defend myself
against an attack
designed to destroy me.

good anger springs
from self-respect
and unites. It tells
me where I am and
asserts my right
to be there.

There is no fear worse
than that of not doing
what I assume others expect.

Live from the inside out . . . not outside in.

We often respond
the way we "should" feel
rather than the way we "do" feel.

for so long. He's asked us to face that "vulture" squarely in the eye and ask: Where is it written? Where's the evidence? Is there proof? Show me the facts? What's so awful? How come things "should" only go your way? Is the present behavior realistic? Is it doing you good? Can you learn more successful ways? We need to stop thinking in terms of "musts." "Musturbation is self-abuse." Albert says that people are disturbed not so much by actual events and persons, as by the views that they take of them. He calls this "shouldhood" — the constant cognitive repetition of shoulds, oughts, and musts that causes us to suffer much pain and anguish when things do not meet our expectations.

Once I've become involved with people, it is, as I see it, my obligation to help them look at what they are doing and to evaluate it, not to tell them to change. It is important to note that if I impose my judgment at this point, I take away the responsibility of the individual. I'm always saying, in effect, "I can't tell you what to do, but I can help you when you decide. I can help you look at your behavior. I *can* say that if you persist with your present behavior nothing will change, and more than likely the consequences will repeat or get worse." In AA we get this message across by appending the word "YET" to any claim that things aren't so bad: "I haven't lost my job — yet, my spouse — yet, my house — yet. I haven't been to jail — yet, been to the hospital — yet, had D.T.'s — yet."

Many people at first refuse to give up the past. There is seemingly no reason why they should; indeed, it may even be rewarding to stay there. Painstakingly, we look at the consequences again and again. We continue the dialogue to get away from "It should not be that way" and toward what would be "possible." At this stage I'm working to get a person to reject irresponsible behaviors and to at least look at the possibility of alternative ways. Remember, this is the "Maybe I can" — critical, vital stage.

Now we reach the other, more hopeful and expansive definition of "responsibility." As we begin to take charge of our lives, we can enjoy being ourselves and can make life meaningful, within the range of responsible behavior.

I know of no one who has written more thoroughly on the concept of responsibility than Bill Glasser, one of my significant gurus whose concepts have been a way of life, rather than just "techniques," for me and those I work with. He defines responsibility, you will recall, as "the ability to fulfill one's needs ... in a way that does not deprive others of their ability to fulfill their needs," as well as the ability to accept the consequences of one's own actions. This notion does not imply self-centeredness, but rather embodies concern, consideration, and respect for the needs and feelings of others. It does not mean the famous quotation of Fritz Perls:

> I do my thing and you do yours,
> I am not in this world to live up to your expectations,
> And you are not in this world to live up to mine.
> I am I, and you are you;
> And if by chance we find each other
> It's beautiful,
> If not, it cannot be helped.

It more closely parallels the rebuttal to Perls' quote from Walter Tubbs which originally appeared in the *Journal of Humanistic Psychology*, Winter 1974.

BEYOND PERLS

> If I just do my thing and you do yours,
> We stand in danger of losing each other
> And ourselves.
>
> I am not in this world to live up to your expectations;
> But I am in this world to confirm you
> As a unique human being,
> And to be confirmed by you.
>
> We are fully ourselves only in relation to each other;
> The I detached from a Thou
> Disintegrates.
>
> I do not find you by chance;
> I find you by an active life
> Of reaching out.
>
> Rather than passively letting things happen to me,
> I can act intentionally to make them happen.
>
> I must begin with myself, true;
> But I must not end with myself;
> The truth begins with two.

Values Clarification

Most people, up until they reach the "Maybe I can" stage, haven't stopped to think about what they're doing and have been blocked from considering that there are other, more positive ways of behaving. They're like Edward Bear in *Winnie the Pooh:*

> Here is Edward Bear, coming downstairs now, Bump, Bump, Bump on the back of his head behind Christopher Robin. It is, as far as he knows, the only way of coming downstairs, but sometimes he feels that there really is another way, if only he could stop bumping for a moment and think of it . . .

One way I try to aid people in evaluating their present behavior is by opening things up with questions. I ask, "What are or will be the natural consequences — natural because you have the choice of doing what will not directly bring on those consequences — of your behavior? How is what you are doing helping? Is there more to life than what you are doing? Are there other ways? Like what?" This is what Bill Glasser calls the "Value Judgment" and what Sid Simon calls "Values Clarification." It is what St. Benedict asked the people to do. He asked them not to just say, but, more important, *do* what they believed in their hearts. We should not simply act upon the wishes of our wife, husband, child, teacher, or boss. Our actions should be based on our own feelings and thoughts. For a long time, I went for therapy to please others rather than to help myself, and naturally therapy didn't do me any good.

Sid Simon's "Values Clarification" approach simply asks, "Does what we do match what we say our values are, and can we look at the gaps between our deeds and our creeds? Is our present behavior a matter of free choice, or is it a habitual and unthinking response to the past?" Our goal is to "clean up" the inconsistencies — if we choose to. The other gurus also give us some tools to do that. Bill Glasser shows how it is impossible to change self-defeating behavior until we truly value and desire that change. Albert Ellis, with his Rational-Emotive Therapy, complements Simon's experiential approach by

there is
no such thing as
best
in a world of
individuals.

"picking the brain" to get at faulty cognitions, such as the ones that turn objectively difficult situations into subjectively "impossible" ones. But Sid really "hits me" repeatedly with the question, "What do I want to do?" His books (most of which are available in inexpensive paperback editions) contain hundreds of ideas on how to get in touch with this part of ourselves. His value-clarification exercises bring alive all these issues in a very practical way, rather than just theorizing about them, and they touch virtually every corner of our emotions and behavior.

Alternatives

The purpose of Values Clarification is to give us alternatives and help us choose among them. Alternatives are what we must have if we are to change.

There are many techniques and devices that I use to open people to alternatives. Here is a sample exercise I often do in groups: Write on a piece of paper in one or two sentences a problem in your life that "has no solution." You've been over it a thousand times, but there is "no answer." The reason there is no answer is that we are so blinded, and we so limit our imagination, that we close out possibilities of change. We simply block out alternatives. Therefore, without the restrictions of time, space, training, money, or other people, I ask you, *without evaluation* (a really difficult task, because the mind keeps flashing what's wrong with each alternative), to list in five or ten minutes all the alternatives — crazy or sane, totally out of space or very real.

For example, suppose the problem is, "I am overweight and wish to lose thirty pounds, so that I might be more physically attractive and healthier." The answers might be: stay fat, Mayo Clinic Diet, Stillman Water Diet, Weight Watchers, Overeaters' Anonymous, wire my mouth, go to a fat farm, etc.

Now for the evaluation of the alternatives. One of Bill Glasser's associates (I'm sorry I can't remember which one) devised five categories for these alternatives. Put each of your alternatives into one of these categories:

1. Most likely — the easiest alternative, that is, continue "as is." This is the Charlie Brown answer: "No problem is so big or so small that I can't run away from it."

2. Most desirable — the "Magic Wand" solution. (I want to lose thirty pounds. I go to sleep tonight, and the Fat Fairy comes and takes the thirty pounds away.)

3. Most probable — just as implied in the word "probability." There is better than a 50/50 chance for success of the alternative. (Weight Watchers, any reasonable diet.)

4. Most possible — it "might work." There is less than a 50/50 chance for success. (A "fad" diet to lose ten pounds the first week.)

5. Most undesirable — most unpleasant. (Sew up my jaw for six months so that I can eat only liquids.)

I have seen over and over that if you really do this, if you just let your imagination run wild, you can "joggle" your head and start to look at ideas that just might not be so far-fetched.

Plan of Action

It is indeed a courageous task to clarify our system of values and wants, but it is not sufficient. In order to correct faulty behavior, we must be willing to act. Thus Sid Simon confronts us with questions such as, "What am I willing to do?" "What am I willing to be?" "Am I willing to take responsibility for my valued actions?" In effect, "How highly and to what degree do I value my values?"

For a value to be mine, I must own it, and therefore accept the consequences of my behavior. For this reason Sid Simon stresses the necessity of acknowledging the anticipated consequences of chosen actions. If, for example, a marketing executive has decided that he prefers carpentry to the boredom of a desk job, he must be willing to accept a less luxurious life-style and lower social status. If an individual makes a decision that a single life is preferable to a tenuous marriage, he must face the fact of loneliness, solitude, and perhaps even dirty laundry. If I am to "own" a value, my actions must be consistent with that value. For instance, an alcoholic

the
booze
that
leaves you
breathless
also leaves you
careless
homeless
family-less
and
jobless .

How easy it is to talk of the past
and the future,
and how difficult to talk
of the here and now.

It's not hard to stop drinking.
It's hard to stay stopped.

Guilt is in the past;
anxiety is in the future.
Where is your mind now?

who has decided that he values his family above the consumption of alcohol cannot merely stop drinking on weekends or for Lent. His abstinence must be consistent with his stated preference.

Thus, after we've considered all the possible alternatives and the consequences of each, we must choose the plan of action we wish to pursue. The plan often comes out of a brainstorming session where we come up with as many ideas as we can (problems are, after all, the absence of ideas) and evaluate each of these plans according to how well it meets the needs of the person or persons concerned. A plan gets a plus if it meets a particular need, a minus if it doesn't, and the plan that gets the most pluses and fewest minuses is the one we choose. But first we have to make sure that we're approaching the problem in terms of the needs that we have, and not the prior solutions that we've been trying to enact all along — and that are thus part of the problem!

For example, a person may think the *solution* is to find a marriage mate, when his or her *need* at this time is to have someone to share thoughts and experiences with. There may be a parent-child conflict where a parent refuses to allow a child to have soda in his room. Although this is the parent's solution, her need, upon a closer look, is not to have the furniture stained. In this case both parties' needs can be met in another way, as by giving the child coasters or putting a protective covering on the furniture.

According to Bill Glasser, it is our job as "helpers" to make the plan small enough to be realistic but large enough to be rewarding — in other words, to try to ensure that the plan doesn't fail, because the people we're dealing with sure have been experts in failure. We always make "Do" plans, not "Don't" plans. We need to keep plans in an affirmative, positive context because we need lessons in success, not failure. So we avoid complex plans. We can always increase the complexity as we achieve success. We make small plans so that we can recognize, reward, and support the smallest achievement. We are goal-oriented, but with moderate, progressively rising goals. We don't talk about being sober forever, but about being sober for six months, one month, one week, one day, whatever is appropriate. Meeting any of these goals is an accomplishment, and we seek to gain strength from cumulative accomplishment.

Commitment to Act

To develop a plan is not enough. We must make an honest commitment to act on it. You and I are funny people. We say one thing and then prove another. We talk the talk, but don't walk the walk. We don't always put our money where our mouth is. Sometimes we do mean it, but self-defeating "people, places, and things" take over. If we're trying to lose weight, for example, we wind up spending the weekend in Hershey, Pennsylvania, locked in a Breyer Ice Cream factory.

Jules Feiffer comically illustrates this point in his cartoons, which raise the issue of commitment and generally wind up with the idea of waiting rather than doing, and of letting things *happen* rather than *acting.*

Well-intentioned as we all are, it is crucial to check whether a person has made a real commitment to a plan. Some of the questions I use to check the commitment are: Is this really important to the person? Does he or she want to put time, effort, and pain into it? How much? What are the obstacles? Is there sufficient involvement? Most important of all, I ask, "What will prevent you from doing the plan?" If there is the slightest hesitation, the slightest "I'll try" or "I sure might do it," then I know we don't really have a commitment, and the plan is probably doomed to failure.

People *already know* the problems that will prevent them from carrying out the plan. That's why they say, "If . . . " or "I'll try." When they do, I ask, "Why not? What could go wrong?" And I keep asking until I get the full answer. If there is a party coming up where a person is likely to drink, or overeat, let's make sure we have a commitment not to drink or overeat *at that party.* Let's bring these things out into the open, talk about them, and clear them up before we go further. Let's not be like the townspeople in "The Emperor's New Clothes," in the sense that by not acknowledging problems we know will

If = I wish.

Deal with facts . . . don't fight them.

I am not a victim of circumstances;
I am a creator of circumstances.

The things you least want
to tell someone about yourself
will help the most.

happen, we conspire to let them happen. Commitment is either 100 percent or zero. At this point, there is no slight case of pregnancy. It makes no sense to go ahead with a plan that is doomed. There is no benefit to be gained from a plan that is going to have built-in failure.

The written contract. Since it takes a Philadelphia lawyer to anticipate all the ways people can defeat themselves, a written contract is an appropriate instrument for trying to ensure commitment. People "forget," so it's a good idea to write the commitment down. People "forget," so we write out, "all booze, not just vodka, scotch, etc., but beer and wine included." This contract, if we have one, is brief but specific. Outlining what each of us is to do, it gets down to the when, where, with whom, and by what steps, and it is signed both by the client and by myself. It may say that you will go to three AA meetings in the next week, and that before you miss a meeting or take a drink you must contact me — and you must reach me, not just try my number once or twice. Its purpose is not so much to make sure the plan is enacted as to confront all those little self-defeating behaviors in advance. I have included a sample contract form on the following page.

Follow-up Support

Acting on the plan is not always an easy task. It can be a very painful new step. The best analogy I know to describe the dichotomy of feelings that occurs is that of the "Siamese Twin" — one wants to change, the other prefers to stay where he is — as presented in the novel *The Drunks* by Donald Newlove. This novel is not only an accurate, incisive dramatization of alcoholism and AA, but also an excellent portrayal of the conflict over change between alcoholic Siamese twins. The story symbolizes the turmoil within one individual as he struggles with both parts of himself during a period of change. Some people, in fact, are not ready to make a change of behavior right away and can only handle the involvement. In these cases, the plan, the commitment can merely be to meet again.

The Contract

The most important thing you do in the program is to write this contract ... it's personal ... it's a deep commitment on your part that you're serious, well-intentioned and ready to change.

Complete the following form. Be as complete as possible. Commit your plan to paper. List all those whom you will enlist in your effort. Leave no one out ... not even those you now don't like. Take your time but don't dawdle.

What is your primary change effort?   Be specific.

Who will help you achieve it?

What steps are necessary to reach the goal? (List in order)

What conditions will exist so you know the goal has been reached?

When will you start?   Finish?   Where and when are the audit points?

How much will it cost in time, money?

Date   _____

Witnessed by   _____

Signed   _____

Throughout the entire process the "validation" and "support" from Chapter Four come into play. At our next contact (whether in person or by phone) we review the contract and see how much of it has been met. Even if it has not all been met, I give strong encouragement and approval where it has been. No one leaves my office without my pointing out something positive that has been achieved, some small change for the better, whether it is in a person's appearance, manner, or observed or reported behavior. This is not superficial, back-slapping good cheer, but specific positive reinforcement. As we "reward" someone, that person starts to reward himself or herself and to build that needed confidence and self-esteem. S/he starts killing those ugly "vultures."

There is still, however, despite all our efforts to ensure otherwise, the possibility that the plan will not work. Note, the *plan* fails, not the *person*. Some failure is inevitable as we change and grow, and therefore we should be prepared to accept failure without the need for excuses. I have the right to fail without necessarily being a "failure." We are simply faced with the question, What should we do now? We can either devise a new plan or redo the old plan.

According to Glasser, if there is little progress or change, either the involvement is insufficient, the value judgment has not been made, or one has bitten off more than one can chew in designing the plan. None of this is reason to punish someone. A person's behavior has its own natural consequences, and we don't have to add to them with more negative reinforcement. It is, however, important for people to experience these consequences and to know that their only excuse is themselves, for they alone are responsible for their behavior.

My responsibility as a "helper" is not to give up. Things didn't work out, but I'm eager to know what we are going to do now. Yesterday is nowhere. Today is the issue. You decided to change your commitment, change your plan. OK. Where do we go from here? Sometimes failure is a kind of test of a "helper's" involvement: Do I really care or will I disappear, as everyone else has, when times get rough? In the beginning of our relationship I made a promise, and I'll stick by that. Neither from others nor from myself will I accept excuses, in large or small matters. If someone doesn't show for an appointment or call me at an appointed time, I'll call him or her. I don't ask for an excuse, but merely inquire, "How are things?" I *give* and *demand* the same respect in "caring" and in "involvement" as that to which friends are entitled.

The important thing is not to think in terms of global success or failure, but of constant effort, evaluation, and progress measured in terms of short-range goals. Every session has its purpose and its goals, and everything that is established in our hour together must be reinforced during the week. Practice builds self-esteem and confidence, and repetition is the soul of learning. Albert Ellis recommends assigning homework between sessions, be it reading a book or article, completing a project, or testing a new behavior. At our next meeting we discuss these assignments. It may sound like casual conversation, but it is purposeful talk. If you were assigned to go to the movies, what did you see? What did it mean to you? If you were assigned to mix with people at a social gathering, with whom did you talk? What was the conversation like? What did you do when it stopped?

A technique I have borrowed from Sid Simon is known as the "Weekly Inventory." It is a simple procedure that involves answering questions such as the following:

Weekly Reaction Sheet

Week of _____

1. **Highpoints**

2. **Lowpoints**

3. **Plans for future events**

4. **Week could have been better**

5. Changes to contract for

6. Open comment

7. The most exciting "happening" of this past week was . . .

8. The most boring activity was . . .

9. I disagreed with . . .

10. I learned that . . .

11. I was bewildered when . . .

12. I felt good about . . .

13. As a result of what I learned this week . . .

It can be beneficial to employ this exercise even on a daily basis. The "Weekly Inventory" asks relevant here-now questions, highlights the need for plan-making, allows for no excuses, and gives a person something to look forward to. As attested to by Victor Frankl, eminent psychiatrist and ex-concentration camp inmate, people (especially those who are institutionalized or suicidal) have a deep need to have something to look forward to, something to live for.

Reading and writing are important tools of change. I'm not doing psychological "mumbo jumbo." What I do as a "helper" can be understood by anyone. I want to share my gurus, and I want others to share theirs. This is really an educational process. It's therapy as reeducation. As part of my reeducation, I have for several years kept journals containing news clippings, quotations from books, films, and other sources, and thoughts and

Selfishness
is
inherently
neither
good nor bad

whether it
nourishes
or injures
depends
on the way
we are selfish

reflections of my own. My journals are an invaluable source of learning to me, and I recommend the idea to you.

A Dialogue

As I review my sharing relationships and reflect upon the messages that I "hear" over and over again, I discover many commonalities. What people have been saying to me is:

I really know I can't get all I want. (If I'm lucky I'll get what I need.)

Let me know you and what values you have.

I lose trust when you start to judge me and my values.

Try to be consistent in your words and actions. Follow through on "contracts."

Only make promises you can keep.

Talk to me. When you are aloof or talk down to me, I feel like a child.

Help me see how my plans might not work out, without giving me the plan. Help me experience success rather than failure.

Teach me to be good to myself and not to condemn myself.

Insist on my personal responsibility. Teach me not to make excuses.

Give me honest answers to my questions.

Admit when you are wrong. Show me that you are not perfect or infallible.

Keep our communications open between our appointments, and I will not abuse your time.

I need lots of strokes and validation. Recognize my achievements and assets. I've been a "failure" for so long that I need help in even seeing success in myself.

I learn more from you as a model than as a critic.

Love me, care for me, nourish me, even when it may be difficult for you to do so.

And I, as a "helper," have been saying:

You, and no one else, are responsible for your behavior.

Responsibility breeds happiness.

Unhappiness does not mean you can act irresponsibly.

Not everything goes the way you think it "should."

You are going to have anxiety and fears. It's really scary to grow and try new things, but the fear and anxiety will pass.

The avoidance of facing life's difficulties and responsibilities is just that — avoidance. Short-term discomfort is better than long-term pain.

There is no Wizard of Oz. You are the wizard.

You and I aren't always going to have all the answers.

You and I aren't always going to be 100 percent competent, intelligent, and achieving.

The past cannot be changed or forgotten. It can only be seen as having taken place. "Now what?" If it is a problem today, it's because you believe it to be. You are only affected by the ideas you *still* believe.

You can't and I can't control things and people. You can only control you.

You can control your emotions by questioning, challenging, and contradicting your beliefs.

We are imprisoned only by ourselves. I spent much time in a worse "prison" than many of my friends who were behind prison bars, for I was in the prison of my mind, and the "guards" were my Vultures.

chapter five exercises

1. Unfinished Business
Write a letter discussing some "unfinished business" you have with someone. Then, putting yourself in that person's position, answer the letter as he or she might.

Would it be possible to finish this "unfinished business" by actually dealing with the person?

2. Try the **Weekly Inventory** suggested in the text.

3. Controllers
Think of those things in your life over which you feel others have control and you don't. Make a list of those "controllers" using the statement:

"I can't (behavior) because of (name of other people, places, things)."

Change your statements to:

"I choose not to (behavior) because of (name of other people, places, things)."

4. Discovery Statements:

I learned that _____

_____

_____

I relearned that _____

_____

I was surprised that _____

_____

_____

I was delighted that _____

_____

_____

I was saddened that _____

_____

_____

I need to _____

_____

_____

What meaning do your "discoveries" have for you?

_____

_____

_____

_____

_____

_____

_____

_____

_____

_____

_____

_____

_____

I love people
when I love them
for being people
and not for
being
young or old
beautiful
hip
wealthy
or
whatever.

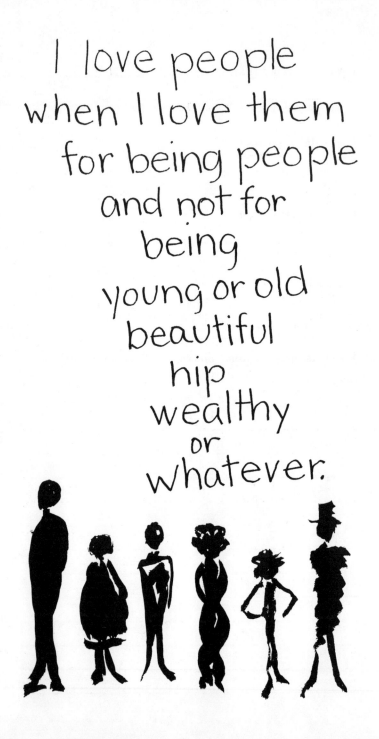

six

Breaking the Silence

This chapter concerns group techniques. Every group, like every individual, is unique. It is a living thing. No principles or prescriptions can replace your sensitivity to the evolving needs and possibilities of the group. There are, however, certain approaches which, while extremely varied in their applications, I have found to be effective in almost all groups.

Many of these are, of course, the same techniques I recommended in the previous chapter for self-development and individual counseling. Since the goals of therapy are the same whether it is conducted individually or collectively, the ideas of gurus Sid Simon, Bill Glasser, and Albert Ellis are equally relevant to the group context. The difference is that the members of a group are all "helpers" for each other. That can be a complication or a tremendous resource for involvement and growth. In seeking to bring out the positive potential of group involvement, I have found various art forms to be uniquely valuable tools. Because the arts fit so well into the group situation and are so often decisive there, I am discussing them here in this chapter on groups. But they can be just as valuable on a one-to-one basis in helping people "open up," clarify their values, and act constructively, as shown by the illustrative quotations from songs and poems and stories that have appeared throughout this book.

The Sounds of Silence

The major psychological crisis of recent history is that caused by alienation and isolation. Eclipsed and imprisoned by technology, detached from our ethnic past and cultural history, we search for identity and for the validation that once accompanied individual creative effort. Paul Simon's lines are a classic expression of the contemporary malaise:

And in the naked light I saw
Ten thousand people maybe more,
People talking without speaking
People hearing without listening,
People writing songs that voices never share,
And no one dares disturb the sound of silence.

The obvious question which arises is, "Is there no reparative process by which we may escape our sense of desolation and isolation, and integrate ourselves with others and our society?" The need for union, integration, and involvement with others is evident in the incredible affinity for group activity that exists in America today. Group therapy, encounter groups, T-groups, ad infinitum seem to be a reaction (perhaps overreaction) to the "ills" of modern society.

The situation becomes confounded, however, when people form a group and find not a group, but a collection of isolated individuals. Anyone who has attended any sort of group function is well acquainted with the uneasiness and lack of trust that are prevalent in a newly formed group. Those who expect to walk off the streets of distrust and alienation into a group situation and find a magic land of love and openness are in for a terrible shock. Are not the individuals in the group the same as those in the streets? Trust and involvement, unfortunately, do not just happen; they take time to build and form. These qualities require what Warren Bennis calls "an unfreezing process," which necessarily is slow and precise.

The emotional states of group members are not unlike the men on a chessboard. Initially contrary to each other, only well into the game do they confront and integrate with each other in some uneven and scattered fashion. An unfortunate consequence of this long process of trust-building and integration is not only that many groups do not have time to complete the process, because of

the things you least
want to tell someone
about yourself
will help the most.

Passion is a noisy thing.

Love lives quietly.

Compliments scare me . . .

I am afraid of getting something that can be subsequently taken away . . .

I am afraid of being put on the spot and now must watch my actions to keep "him" thinking this way about me. There is a part of me that knows I am not as good as his compliment implies. Also, I have often been insincere when making similar compliments.

We grew into what we are
through relationships with people. ,
We grow into what we can be
through relationships with people.

contractual and other limitations, but also that members quickly lose faith and thus interest in the group long before even the most superficial involvement has a chance to occur. To keep pace with modern man's impatience, we need a quick and simple method by which a leader or facilitator can hasten integration and mutual involvement.

Art as an Integrative Force

I along with other group leaders have searched for a method that would bring together and integrate all kinds of people with all kinds of problems. It seemed an impossible task, like trying to mix oil and water. Finally, a few of us stumbled on the idea of using literature, music, poetry, and all the arts to help achieve involvement in all types of group settings. This method not only enhanced group interaction, but also could be used to highlight the very notions I was stressing (choice, responsibility, value judgments, and so on). It could involve all types of people, with every type of problem, in any type of group. I have, therefore, tried to combine the ideas of my three major gurus — Simon, Glasser, Ellis — with the words of literature, music, and poetry, as a way by which we may form group involvement, seek self-knowledge, and discover our identities.

There is nothing more universal than the arts. Literature, music, drama, art, and the theatre have, since the beginning of time, been a key element in cultural unity. But true art transcends even the culture. The drama of Shakespeare, the music of the Italian Renaissance, the ancient art of Egypt, the comedy of Aristophanes are all examples of art that have not only bridged cultures, but also the limits of time and history.

Art is universal because it touches everyone. It externalizes even the deepest feelings and thoughts, therefore stressing the commonalities rather than the differences among each and every member of the human race. Shakespeare captured the essence of this feeling in *Love's Labour's Lost:* "They are the books, the arts, the academic, that show, contain and nourish the world." There is a definite connection between the disciplines of

Another person's behavior is "bad"
or "understandable" according to
my experience with MYSELF.

My criticism of him amounts to:
"If I had said that or acted that way,
I would think of myself as selfish,
opinionated, immature, etc."

Don't analyze me — understand me.

psychology, psychiatry, sociology, anthropology, and philosophy and the arts. As Bill Glasser says, "Both old and modern legends, plays, and literature abound with examples of abnormal psychology, from *Oedipus Rex* through *Hamlet* to the tortured Blanche Dubois in Tennessee Williams' *A Streetcar Named Desire*. Every type of deviant human behavior has been richly chronicled in literature, often more accurately than in scientific works." One finds that through literature, through poetry, through music, and indeed through all the arts, a way can be found to ignite emotion and involvement in even the most atomized groups.

I have found the use of prose a successful tool in aiding group involvement. The method simply involves having a person read a literary passage, section or entire work that applies to his emotional frame, or to the issue at hand in the group. Many studies have been done using literature as the basis for group interaction, and the usefulness of the process seems fairly well established. I have used the technique with all kinds of groups with a high degree of success.

Poetry is also a tool that I have found beneficial. J.J. Leedy, an eminent psychiatrist, in his books *Poetry the Healer* and *Poetry Therapy*, has documented the success of using poetry in many different group situations. Not only is it helpful to read poetry in groups, but if group members also actually write and share their own creative efforts, involvement is greatly accelerated.

Finally, there is no language more universal than music. The sounds and lyrics of contemporary music, including rock, folk, jazz, and country and western styles, all accurately portray the situation, the feelings, the dilemma of modern man. Many classical pieces also create specific moods and atmospheres that lend themselves to emotional sharing. All music is a valuable medium for the group experience. It speaks not only with words, but also with sounds and vibrations.

Each of the universal art forms possesses the power to bring a group together and allows for early integration and involvement among its members. The skepticism and mistrust of an infant group quickly diminishes when each member can feel and share the confusion of Hamlet, the pain of Billie Holiday, or even the joyfulness, yet irresponsibility, of Peter Pan, and relate it to his own life and the lives of other members of the group.

In my work at local clinics I found that characteristically uptight groups begin to laugh, weep or get angry where there was, shortly before, a total lack of emotion. So I use these techniques to get people involved with people. My first major experience using the arts occurred at the Blue Hills Clinic, where I was running a group consisting of alcoholics of every race, color, and creed, most of whom were not particularly pleased to be there. When I introduced music into the group, it elicited responses from previously uncommunicative individuals. An aliveness was born in that group that had never occurred before. Another example is that of an outpatient group which included some rough and tumble, uncommunicative "graduates" of local correctional institutions, who practically reacted violently when I passed around a copy of The Velveteeen Rabbit (a children's book on caring, being real, and so on), passages of which were to be read aloud by each member of the group. As one might expect, progress was at first slow, but the result was a true involvement with the issues brought up in the book. In many other groups people have become so involved and interested in the experience of the group that they have been more than willing to write their own creative works and to allow them to be experienced and discussed by the group. In the past two years, with this type of group, I can honestly say that attendance approached 100 percent, an operational measure of success by anyone's yardstick.

Group Involvement and the Arts

The basic advantage of the group setting is that it provides a place where people can get "involved" with other people. This involvement is a basic theme of both Sid Simon and Bill Glasser, who make suggestions for cultivating interaction among group members. The "helper" in such a group refuses to keep analytic distance. On the contrary, s/he is a leader and model for sharing and risk-taking. It is through the leader's example that the group members evolve a caring and nourishing atmosphere that both Simon and Glasser deem necessary for true integration of human beings.

One stipulation of group procedure, therefore, is the personalization of statements, or the "I-me" focus. When commenting on a particular passage of literature or music, for instance, the group members must make all references in the first person. When a speaker owns his or her statements and emotions, not only will s/he stay in touch with and take responsibility for his or her feelings, but other group members may directly experience those feelings and thereby be encouraged to take risks in sharing their own emotions.

Another stipulation involves keeping conversation on a "here-now" level. The literature or music used is designed to give the readers or listeners emotional stimulation and thus insight into their own feelings. The emotional experience, which is happening in the present, is a much more potent stimulus to involvement when kept in the "here-now" reference frame than when cast in "there-then" references. A tear shed for Willy Loman in *Death of a Salesman*, when tied in with familial and moral issues that have immediate impact on a person's life, has an infinitely greater impact on other group members than a discussion of these issues in light of a person's pathological condition and the possible source of that condition.

Still another stipulation is that group members offer nourishing comments and suggestions instead of the blatant criticism practiced in many groups today. If, for example, a group member has truly decided that he values the love of his wife and family above his love for consumption of alcohol, then supportive, yet nonjudgmental recommendations of AA or Antabuse treatment programs will obviously have a much more reinforcing effect than a mere condemnation of the person's destructive behavior. One group member, a totally hostile, uncommunicative adolescent, after learning involvement in the group, not only improved his outlook and showed greater interest in school, but also wrote a series of poems which he openly shared with the group (an incredible feat for even a so-called "well-adjusted" 17-year-old):

> . . . I can't do what they say
> And Lord knows I've tried
> And when I do what they say
> I feel wrong deep inside.
> What am I supposed to do
> Do I know what I think right
> And live the rest of my life in fright
> Do I do what I think is right
> And be mad at myself
> That I didn't put up with that . . .

Values Clarification and the Arts

When we reach the stage of values clarification, our gurus offer exercises specifically adapted to the group context, so that the effectiveness of the process can be enhanced by mutual involvement and participation. Albert Ellis urges that group members join with the "helper" in attacking faulty cognitions that support self-defeating behavior. Bill Glasser proposes techniques such as group brainstorming of alternatives. And Sid Simon has devised exercises through which group members can not only share and integrate their feelings with each other, but also offer each other viable alternatives.

There is no greater aid in clarifying and judging values than the arts. Sid Simon himself makes use of the poetry of James Kavanaugh and the comic routines of Shelley Berman (such as "Right, Shirley?"). Through the characters of literature and lyrics of music the group members recognize and relate directly to the issues with which they are dealing. There is a true "coming to life" of their faulty cognitions, their faulty behaviors, their muddled values right before their eyes and ears. Those dealing with negative identity, self-esteem and goal-orientation can't help but shudder when in the company of Willy Loman in Arthur Miller's *Death of a Salesman*. Group members dealing with marriage or divorce and the issue of "the inability to live with you and the inability to live without you" stiffen in the company of *Virginia*

Woolf. Who among us is not, indeed, very often *Waiting for Godot*?

One group member, Marilyn, shared her identification with a poem which she read to her group. It's from *Song of the Open Road* by Walt Whitman:

Alone, whoever you are
Come travel with me.
Traveling with me you find one never tires.
The Earth never tires
The Earth is rude and incomprehensible at first
Be not discouraged.
Keep on
There are divine things well enveloped
I swear to you there are divine things more beautiful than
    words can tell.
Alone we must not stop here however sweet these laid up
    stores however convenient this dwelling
We cannot remain here.
However sheltered this port
And however calm these waters
We must not anchor here.
However welcome this hospitality that surrounds us
We are permitted to receive it but a little while.

"I linked into a lot of feelings about leaving school, for one thing," Marilyn explained. "I seemed to be there, and I 'hooked' into the growth process. The poem for me talks about a lot of promise for new discoveries in myself. If I can take that first step, and risk and grow a little bit, once the process starts I really won't stop myself. I can try to delude myself, but I know once I start growing I have to keep on with that process.

"So this means a lot to me right now, and it meant a lot to the group. I had a feeling with this poem, that if I can make the selection and gear it to where the group is at, I can really get a lot of input and feedback."

Another reaction to group sharings of literature is that of Peter:

"One of the things we said that really struck me was that feeling that you are not alone. A lot of the feelings that I thought were just within my own head, I found out were really shared by a lot of other people.

"I brought in, just for this group, *Escape from Freedom* by Erich Fromm, and I thought I would read a couple of passages that explained how I would think that this would be applicable to a group that I counsel.

"Fromm talks about modern man living under the illusion that he knows what he wants when he actually knows what he is supposed to want. In order to accept this, we have to realize that to know what one really wants is not as easy as most people think. One of the most difficult problems I have is to answer a question I frantically try to avoid by accepting ready-made goals as though they were my own; and it is something that I know I have to wrestle with once in awhile. What do I really want, as opposed to what other people have told me that I really want?

"Fromm finds the answer in what he calls positive freedom, which, he says, implies the principle that there is no higher power than the unique individual self. That man is the center and purpose of his life and that the growth and realization of man's individuality is an end which can never be subordinated to the purposes that are supposed to have greater dignity. I guess that is the answer that I am trying to find in myself. Trying to realize that there isn't any higher power than myself. That what I do has got to come basically from me. This is something where it can mean a lot to get support and help from other group members who are all going through the same kind of struggles and can help me by sharing. That way, I know that I am not alone."

Children's books also provide a vast repertoire for the "helper." Human feelings are not confined to the most elaborate literary resources, but are just as richly chronicled in children's novels. You will remember the example given earlier of Edward Bear in *Winnie-the-Pooh*, who comes down the stairs "bump, bump, bump, on the back of his head behind Christopher Robin. It is, as far as he knows, the only way of coming downstairs, but sometimes he feels there really is another way, if only he could stop bumping for a moment and think of it." This seeming inability to change and this habitual pattern of living are experienced by all of us much of the time. Children's novels also may elegantly describe the problems of life and the human condition, as in Margery

Williams' *The Velveteen Rabbit,* which deals with the issue of "becoming real":

> It doesn't happen all at once. It takes a long time. That's why it doesn't often happen to people who break easily, or have sharp edges, or have to be carefully kept. Generally, by the time you are REAL, most of your hair has been loved off, and your eyes drop off, and you get loose in the joints, and very shabby. But these things don't matter at all because once you are REAL, you can't be ugly except to those who don't understand.

Children's books not only have the advantage of being simple enough for almost any member of the group to understand, but are so graphically accurate at stating the human condition that even a group of Greek scholars could gain much from a group based on nothing but Dr. Seuss.

Popular music is also an invaluable source in conveying to people the issues and feelings that affect them most. Gil Scott Heron, in "Living in a Bottle" and "Home is Where the Hatred Is," provokes the alcohol and drug abuser, respectively, to face the actual pain and consequence of his indulgence. Kenny Rankin in "Coming Down" richly expresses the fear and terror of coming down from a bad trip, while Grace Slick in "White Rabbit" supports the use of drugs as a mind expander when she advises the listener to "feed your head." Les McCann and Eddie Harris question the validity of the American standards of life and cultural preferences in "Compared to What?" while Bob Dylan examines the plight of growing up in a jet-age technological society in "Subterranean Homesick Blues." The total listening experience of contemporary music provides the group members not only with topics for discussion, but also for personalizing those issues and relating them to their own value systems and problems.

Listen to Karen, a group member, comment on an album she brought in to share with the group:

"I brought in a song from an album called *Free to be You and Me* by Marlo Thomas and Friends. The whole album is really fantastic. Primarily this was recorded for children. Marlo says on the cover that she has a favorite niece that she had a lot of trouble finding suitable literature for — she just found everything very sex-oriented and very traditional. So she made this album, and I played one of the songs from it called "It's All Right to Cry." I think that really gets down to the feelings that I have had.

"For me, I know I grew up not showing feelings at all and having a smile for a mask, feeling *that* was a show of strength, and this song really hit home for me . . . It is all right to have and show feelings."

It is through this type of literature and music that the group members can objectify and relate to the problems that plague their lives. The arts have the ability to open our eyes and mirror the issues that disrupt our lives. It is infinitely simpler to clarify our values when they are vivified and presented to us in their universal form, as is done through literature and music.

Behavior Change and the Arts

Once values have been clarified and alternatives chosen, decisions have to be acted upon. Thus Sid Simon and Bill Glasser suggest that members publicly affirm to the group not only their values, but their specific commitments to action. Albert Ellis has members report to the group on the homework assignments they have carried out.

Here, too, in the most thrilling and yet most subtle stage of therapy, art can be brought into play. Books such as *Jonathan Livingston Seagull* and movies such as *Man of La Mancha,* with music like "The Impossible Dream," are stimulating, provoking, and often energizing in the struggle to change behavior. The choo-choo train who through sheer stamina and will power repeated, "I think I can, I think I can, I think I can, I think I can . . . " until he reached the summit of the hill provides a descriptive example of the power that prevails through the pain in the battle for freedom, both physical and mental. One group member shared a quote from *Julius Caesar* in which Caesar changed his statement that he was not able to go to the Senate to "I *will not* go to the Senate." This, of course, brought to life the issue of "can't" vs. "won't" e.d the notion that the inability to change behavior is very often a refusal to change behavior.

A Well-Run Group
The therapies of Ellis, Glasser, and Simon complement and supplement each other and provide the leader with everything s/he needs to open up, maintain, and stimulate virtually any type of group. The art forms further elevate these techniques by placing the individual in graphic contact with him- or herself and the issues to be dealt with. They provide a mild shock effect, a descriptive mirror image of each person's own suffering, faulty behaviors, and faulty cognitions. The leader who is prepared with appropriate literature, music, and exercises can use an intuitive sense of appropriateness along with a grab-bag of materials to prod and pry group interaction until, indeed, the group flows and is capable of maintaining itself.

Individual group members are often found at different stages of treatment. One may be making commitments to the entire group, another may for the first time be trying to share an original poem, while a third may still be in the initial stages of forming trust and involvement with the group. Under the theories and techniques I have outlined, each member chooses, from his or her particular vantage point and according to his or her stage of progress, what to share, how much to open up, and where to go next. But s/he is, of course, offered guidance and direction. Through these methods group members may learn early that their feelings are indeed universal and that it is acceptable, even rewarding, to share them with other members of the human race.

chapter six exercises

1. Please — Hear What I'm Not Saying

PLEASE — hear what I'm not saying: Don't be fooled by
the face I wear, for I wear a thousand masks.
And none of them are me. Don't be fooled, for God's sake
don't be fooled.
I give you the impression that I'm secure, That confidence
is my name and coolness is my game. And that I need no
one. But don't believe me. Beneath dwells the real me in
confusion, in fear, in aloneness.
That's why I create a mask to hide behind, to shield me
from the glance that knows, But such a glance is precisely
my salvation. That is, if it's followed by acceptance, if it's
followed by love. It's the only thing that can liberate me
from my own self-built prison walls. I'm afraid that deep-
down I'm nothing, that I'm just no good. And that you will
see this and reject me. And so begins the parade of masks.
I idly chatter to you.
I tell you everything that's really nothing and nothing of
what's everything, of what's crying within me.
Please listen carefully and try to hear what I'm not saying.
I'd really like to be genuine and spontaneous, and me.

But you've got to help me. You've got to hold out your
hand. Each time you're kind, and gentle, and encouraging,
Each time you try to understand because you really care,
my heart begins to grow wings, very feeble wings, but
wings. With your sensitivity and sympathy and your
power of understanding, you alone can release me from
my shadow world of uncertainty — From my lonely
prison. It will be easy for you. The nearer you approach
me, the blinder I may strike back. But I am told that love is
stronger than strong walls. And in this lies my hope, only
hope. Please try to beat down these walls with firm hands.
But gentle hands — for a child is very sensitive. Who am I,
you may wonder? I am someone you know very well. For I

am every man you meet, and I am every woman you meet.
And I am you, also.

—Anonymous

Who are the "good listeners" in your life?

Who hears your hidden words?

Who understands you with little or no words?

What qualities make them good listeners?

If you wanted to get better at listening, what are six things you could do more consistently? (Thanks to Sid Simon.)

2. Art Forms

Make a list of your favorite songs, poems, and books.

What makes them meaningful to you?

Is there a consistent theme running through them?

Let's reflect on the **Discovery Statements** in relation to your favorite art forms.

I learned that _____

_____

_____

I relearned that _____

_____

_____

I was surprised that _____

_____

_____

I was delighted that _____

_____

_____

I was saddened that _____

_____

_____

I need to _____

_____

_____

What meaning do your "discoveries" have for you?

3. Now, in relation to this entire book, I invite you once more to respond to the **Discovery Statements.**

I learned that _____

_____

_____

I relearned that _____

_____

_____

I was surprised that _____

_____

_____

I was delighted that _____

_____

_____

I was saddened that _____

_____

_____

I need to _____

_____

_____

What meaning do your "discoveries" have for you?

_____

_____

_____

_____

_____

If I feel an aversion toward someone
or if I find myself ignoring or turning
away from someone in a group,
I am probably avoiding within myself
what this person represents
that is true about me.

**To reveal myself
honestly and openly
takes the rarest kind of courage.**

Yesterday's pain
may lead to today's understanding,
and thus to hope for tomorrow.

When you drink,
you die a day at a time.
When sober, you live a day at a time.

**After I straighten out how
I think a fault works in someone else,
I can then look at my own
behavior with a new clarity.**

Faith is not a blind leap into nothing,
but a thoughtful walk into the light.

Conclusion

As I sit in Lincoln Center watching Beverly Sills sing in *The Barber of Seville,* I think of all the nearby bars that I used to pass out in. And I remember the struggles and pains that I endured in silent lament — my personal inadequacies, my unrealized and unrealistic aspirations, my feelings of alienation from self and others, my pent-up anger, my unshed tears for all my hurts since childhood. In those days I chose solutions that became problems in themselves. I still have many of the same pains — feelings of inadequacy in close personal relationships, difficulties in balancing leisure and work, the tribulations of sudden illnesses and deaths, and the strains and discontinuities of daily life. But I never think of drinking or other forms of drug-taking as an alternative. I know that every person alive has his own share of these dilemmas. To think that it will ever be otherwise is to deny reality. And so I listen to my gurus and look for constructive alternatives that don't always lessen the pain for the moment, but that on a long-term basis give us the best chance of enjoying the satisfactions and "highs" that we can reasonably hope for.

At my first AA meeting the thing that caught my eye was the sign that read, "You Are Not Alone." You are not alone in suffering, and you are not alone in rebirth. As it has been for me, so may it be for you. If you have chosen some destructive way, you can go back and learn anew, for you have the power to choose and to change. If you can learn to think, "This, too, will pass — as long as I keep working and loving and coping," you will gain the strength of hope and the strength of action.

There are so many resources out there that can help in this relearning: books, art, organizations, and especially people. Take them; they're yours. To the extent that my experience and knowledge enable me to help, I extend to you that experience and knowledge. In the realm of caring and involvement we don't say, "What's mine is mine," but "What's mine is mine — and yours, too."

Bibliography

Here are a few of the books, poems, and songs that I have found useful in my work. I have divided them into two lists: a Reference Bibliography, consisting of works that more or less directly relate, either theoretically or by example, to the ideas in this book; and an expanded list of Works to Experience, i.e., those that I have found stimulating to use in groups, as described in Chapter 6. This second list, especially, is only a small portion of the practically infinite bibliography that might someday be put together. Why don't you pick something relevant from this list, listen to it or read it, and discuss it with the members of your group, your family, your friends. Also, if you have found any books or records to be particularly useful and don't see them on my list, why don't you jot them down and send them to me so that I might make my list more complete.

A. Reference Bibliography

Addeo, Edmond G.; and Jovita R., *Why Our Children Drink*, Hudson, Wis., Prentice Hall 1975

Anonym, Kenneth, *Understanding the Recovering Alcoholic*, Canfield, Ohio, Alba Books 1974

Baars, Conrad W., M.D. *Born Only Once*, Chicago, Franciscan Herald Press 1975

Bach, George R.; Deutsch, Ronald M., *Pairing*, NY, Peter Wyden, Inc. 1970

Bach, George R.; Goldberg, Herb, *Creative Aggression*, Garden City, NY, Doubleday and Co., Inc. 1974

Bach, George R.; Wyden, Peter, *The Intimate Enemy*, NY, Avon Books 1975

Bach, Richard, *Jonathan Livingston Seagull*, Riverside, NJ, Macmillan Pub. 1970

Becker, Ernest, *Denial of Death*, NY, Free Press 1973

Berne, Eric, *Games People Play*, NY, Grove Press 1964

Branden, Nathaniel, *Disowned Self*, NY, Nash Publishing Corp. 1972

Caine, Lynn, *Widow*, NJ, William Morrow and Co. 1974

Connolly, Myles, *Mr. Blue*, Garden City, NY, Doubleday and Co., Inc. 1954

Corsini, Raymond J., *Current Psychotherapies*, Itasca, Ill., Peacock, FT Pubs 1973

Crowe, Cecily, *The Twice Born*, NY, Random House 1972

Cullum, Albert, *The Geranium on the Windowsill Just Died but Teacher You Went Right On*, Harlin Quist Publications 1976

DeRosis, Helen, and Pellegrino, Victoria Y., *Book of Hope*, McMillan 1976

Dyer, Wayne W., *Your Erroneous Zones*, Funk & Wagnalls Co. 1976

Ellis, Albert; Harper, Robert A., *New Guide to Rational Living*, N. Hollywood, Calif., Wilshire Book Co. 1975
All of Albert Ellis's other books.

Fort, Joel, *Alcohol*, NY, McGraw-Hill Book Co. 1973

Fort, Joel, *Pleasure Seekers*, Bobbs-Merrill Co., Inc. 1969

Frank, Jerome D., *Persuasion and Healing*, NY, Schocken Paperback 1974

Frankl, Victor, *Man's Search for Meaning*, NY, Pocket Book 1963

Friedman, Myra, *Buried Alive: The Biography of Janis Joplin*, NY, William Morrow and Co. 1973

Fromm, Erich, *The Art of Loving*, Scranton, Pa., Harper and Row 1974

Glasser, William, *The Identity Society*, NY, Harper and Row, 1972

Glasser, William, *Mental Health or Mental Illness*, NY, Perennial Library 1970

Glasser, William, *Positive Addiction*, NY, Harper and Row 1976

Glasser, William, *Reality Therapy*, NY, Harper and Row 1965

Goldman, Albert, *Ladies and Gentlemen . . . Lenny Bruce*, Md., Ballantine Books 1974

Grinder, Michael, *I Am*, Millbrae, Calif., Celestial Arts 1973

Gunther, Bernard, *Sense Relaxation*, Toronto, Macmillan Co. 1968

Gunther, Bernard, *What to Do Until the Messiah Comes*, Toronto, Macmillan Co. 1970

Haley, Jay, *The Power Tactics of Jesus Christ*, NY, Avon Books 1969

Hall, Nancy Lee, *A True Story of a Drunken Mother*, Plainfield, Vt., Daughters Inc. 1974

Hampden-Turner, Charles, *Sane Asylum*, San Francisco, San Francisco Book Co. 1976

Ian, Janis, "Between the Lines"

Ian, Janis, "Stars"

James, Muriel; Jongeward, Dorothy, *Born to Win,* Reading, Ma., Addison-Wesley Pub. Co. 1971

Johnson, David W., *Reaching Out,* Hudson, Wis., Prentice-Hall, Inc. 1972

Johnson, Vernon, *I'll Quit Tomorrow,* NY, Harper and Row 1973

Jourard, Sidney M., *The Transparent Self,* NY, Van Nostrand Reinhold Co. 1971

Jourard, Sidney M.; Overlade, Dan C., *Disclosing Man to Himself,* NY, Van Nostrand Reinhold Co. 1968

Kalant, Harold; Kalant, Oriana, *Drugs, Society and Personal Choice,* Don Mills, Ontario, General Publishing Co. 1971

Kaplan, Eugene H.; Wieder, Herbert, *Drugs Don't Take People, People Take Drugs,* Secaucus, NJ, Lyle Stuart 1974

Kiernan, Thomas, *Shrinks Etc.,* NY, Dial Press, 1974

Kopp, Sheldon B., *Guru,* Palo Alto, Ca., Science and Behavior Books 1971

Kopp, Sheldon B., *If You Meet The Buddha On The Road, Kill Him,* Palo Alto, CA, Science and Behavior Books 1972

Kopp, Sheldon B., *This Side of Tragedy,* Palo Alto, CA, Science and Behavior Press, 1977.

Kubler-Ross, Elisabeth, *On Death and Dying,* Riverside, NJ, Macmillan Pub. 1974

Kuten, Jay, *Coming Together, Coming Apart,* NY, Macmillan Pub. Co. 1974

Leshan, Eda, *The Wonderful Crisis of Middle Age,* NY, McKay 1973

Lewis, Howard R.; Stristfeld, Harold S., *Growth Games,* NY, Bantam Books 1972

Living Sober, AA Publication, Alcoholics Anonymous World Services, Inc. NY 1975

Low, Abraham A., *Mental Health Through Will Training,* N. Quincy, Ma., Christopher Publishing House (Mass) 1974

Luthman, Shirley G., *Intimacy,* Los Angeles, CA, Nash Publishing 1972

Malcolm, Andrew I., *The Craving for the High,* Markham, Ontario, Simon and Schuster of Canada 1975

Maloney, Barbara, *A Sensitive Passionate Man,* NY, McKay 1974

Maloney, Ralph, *Fish In A Stream In A Cave,* NY, Norton 1972

Marin, Peter; Cohen, Allen Y., *Understanding Drug Use,* Scranton, Pa., Harper and Row 1971

Maslow, Abraham H., *Toward a Psychology of Being,* NY, Van Nostrand Reinhold Co. 1968

May, Rollo, *Love and Will,* NY, WW Norton and Co. 1969

McAndrew, Craig; Edgerton, Robert B., *Drunken Comportment,* Chicago, IL, Aldine Publishing 1969

McWilliams, Peter, — series on love

Miller, Arthur, *Death of A Salesman,* NY, Viking Compass Press 1958

Moustakas, Clark — assorted books and articles on loneliness

Newlove, Donald, *The Drunks,* NY, E.P. Dutton and Co. 1974

Newman, Mildred; Berkowitz, Bernard, *How To Be Your Own Best Friend,* NY, Random House 1971

Nouwen, Henri J.M., *Reaching Out,* Garden City, NY, Doubleday and Co. 1975

Nouwen, Henri J.M., *The Wounded Healer,* Garden City, NY, Doubleday and Co. 1972

Oates, Wayne, *Confessions of a Workaholic,* NY, Abingdon Press 1972

Otto, Herbert, Any group material by him.

Paulus, Trina, *Hope For the Flowers,* NY, Newmann Press 1972

Peele, Stanton; Brodsky, Archie, *Love and Addiction,* NY, Taplinger Pub. Co. 1975; NY, New American Library 1976

Pirsig, Robert M., *Zen and The Art of Motorcycle Maintenance,* NY, Bantam 1974

Powell, John, *Fully Human, Fully Alive,* Niles, Ill., Argus Communications 1976

Powell, John, *The Secret of Staying in Love,* Niles, Ill., Argus Communications 1974

Powell, John, *Why Am I Afraid To Love?* Niles, Ill., Argus Communications 1967

Powell, John, *Why Am I Afraid To Tell You Who I Am?* Niles, Ill., Argus Communications 1969

Prather, Hugh, *Notes to Myself,* Moab, Utah, Real People Press 1970

Previn, Dory, "On My Way To Where"

Rogers, Carl R., *On Becoming A Person,* Boston, Mass., Houghton-Mifflin Co. 1961

Rogers, Carl R.; Stevens, Barry, *Person to Person,* Lafayette, Calif., Real People Press, 1967

Saint Exupery, Antoine de, *The Little Prince,* NY, Harcourt, Brace and World Inc. 1943

Satir, Virginia, *Peoplemaking,* Palo Alto, Calif., Science and Behavior Books 1972

Saulnier, Leda; Simard, Terri, *Personal Growth and Interpersonal Relations,* Hudson, Wis., Prentice-Hall, Inc. 1973

Schutz, William C., *Here Comes Everybody,* NY, Harper and Row 1971

Schutz, William C., *Joy,* NY, Grove Press 1969

Scoppettone, Sandra, *The Late Great Me,* NY, AP Putnam 1976

Shain, Merle, *Some Men Are More Perfect Than Others,* NY, Charterhouse 1973

Sheehy, Gail, *Passages,* NY, E.P. Dutton and Co., 1976

Silverstein, Shel, *Where the Sidewalk Ends: Poems and Drawings,* NY, Harper and Row 1972
"Living Tree," "The Missing Piece"

Simon, Sidney B.; Howe, Leland W.; Kirschenbaum, Howard, *Values Clarification,* NY, Hart Publishing Co. 1972 (and anything else by Sidney Simon)

Smith, David E.; Gay, George R. (Eds.), *It's So Good, Don't Even Try It Once,* Englewood Cliffs, NJ, Prentice-Hall 1972

Stevens, Barry, *Don't Push The River,* Moab, Utah, Real People Press 1970

SUFI Literature — Zen

Verny, Thomas, *Inside Groups,* NY, McGraw-Hill Co. 1975

Weinberg, Jon — any and all of his material on alcoholism, available through CompCare Publications, Mpls., MN

Weiner, Jack B., *The Morning After,* NY, Delacorte Press 1973

Williams, Margery, *The Velveteen Rabbit,* Garden City, NY, Doubleday 1958

Yalom, Irvin D., *The Theory and Practice of Group Psychotherapy,* NY, Basic Books, Inc. 1975

Young, Howard S., *A Rational Counseling Primer,* NY, Institute for Rational Living, Inc. 1974

B. Works to Experience

Literature

Abrams et al (Ed.), *The Norton Anthology of English Literature (Vol. 1 & 2)*
Adoff, Arnold (Ed.), *Brothers and Sisters*
Anderson, *I Never Sang for my Father*
Axline, Virginia, *Dibs in Search of Self*
Bach, Richard, *Jonathan Livingston Seagull*
Baum, L. Frank, *Wizard of Oz*
Becker, Ernest, *The Denial of Death*
Beckett, Samuel, *Waiting for Godot*
Bonhan, Frank, *Chief*
Bretall, Robert (Ed.) *A Kierkegaard Anthology*
Brooks, Charlotte (Ed.), *I (Me)*
Brown, Claude, *Manchild in the Promised Land*
Brown, Dee, *Bury My Heart at Wounded Knee*
Buber, Martin, *I and Thou*
Bugental, James F.T. — anything by this fine Humanist psychologist
Buscaglia, Leo, *Love*
Camus, Albert, *The Myth of Sisyphus and Other Essays*
Camus, *The Stranger*
Carroll, L., *Alice in Wonderland*
Cassidy, Bruce, *Iggy*
Castaneda, Carlos, *A Separate Reality*
Cervantes, M. *Don Quixote*
Chesler, Phyllis, *Women and Madness*
Cole, Larry, *Our Children's Keeper*
Crane, S., *Red Badge of Courage*
Crawford, Charles, *Bad Fall*
Crichton, Michael, *Andromeda Strain*
Dickinson, E., *Isolation*
Ferlinghetti, Lawrence, *A Coney Island of the Mind*
Fitzgerald, F. Scott, *The Great Gatsby*
Ford, Edward E., with Zorn, Robert L., *Why Marriage, Why Be Lonely*
Frankl, Viktor, *Man's Search for Meaning*
Fromm, E., *Art of Loving, Revolution of Hope*
Fuller, S., *No More Second Hand God*
Gibran, Kahlil, *Broken Wings*
Gibran, Kahlil, *Tears and Laughter*
Gibran, Kahlil, *The Prophet*
Goethe, Johann, *Faust — Parts I & II*
Golding, William, *Lord of the Flies*
Gregory, Dick, *Nigger*
Gunther, John, *Death Be Not Proud*
Heinlein, Robert, *Stranger in a Strange Land*
Hesse, Hermann, *Demian*
Hesse, Hermann, *Journey to the East*
Hesse, Hermann, *Magister Ludi*
Hesse, Hermann, *Siddhartha*
Hesse, Hermann, *Steppenwolf*
Huxley, A., *Brave New World*
Johnson, Clive, *Vendanta*
Joseph, Stephen, *The Me Nobody Knows*
Josephsons, *Man Alone*
Kafka, Franz, *Parables and Paradoxes*
Kavanaugh, James — any of his books of poetry
Keen, Sam, *To a Dancing God*
Kellogg, Marjorie, *Tell Me That You Love Me, Junie Moon*
Kerouac, Jack, *On the Road*

Kerr, Barbara, *Strong at the Broken Places*
Kesey, Ken, *One Flew Over the Cuckoo's Nest*
Laing, R.D., *Knots*
Marquis, Don, *Archy and Mehitabel*
Maslow, A., *The Third Force*
Maxwell, Ruth, *The Booze Battle*
May, R., *Love and Will*
McKuen, Rod, *Listen to the Warm*
Meeks, John E., M.D., *The Fragile Alliance*
Melville, H., *Moby Dick*
Meriwether, Louise, *Daddy was a Number Runner*
Miller, A., *Death of a Salesman*
Miller, et al, *The Dimensions of the Short Story*
Moore, Carmon, *Somebody's Angel Child: The Story of Bessie Smith*
Neihardt, John, *Black Elk Speaks*
Otto, Herbert and Mann, John (Ed.), *Ways of Growth*
Pirsig, Robert, *Zen and the Art of Motorcyle Maintenance*
Plath, S., *The Bell Jar*
Prather, Hugh, *Notes to Myself*
Radice, Betty and Balduk, Robert (Ed.), *The Bhagavad Gita*
Richette, Lisa, *The Throwaway Children*
Rilke, Rainer, *The Notebooks of Malte Laurids*
Ross, Pat (Ed.), *Young and Female*
Rotter, Pat (ed.), *Bitches and Sad Ladies*
Saint Exupery, A., *The Little Prince*
Salinger, J.D., *Catcher in the Rye*
Sartre, Jean Paul, *The Wall and Other Stories*
Savory, Louis and O'Connor, Thomas (Ed.), *The Heart Has its Seasons: A Reflection on the Human Condition*
Schneider, Elisabeth (ed.), *Poems and Poetry*
Schreiber, Flora, *Sybil*
Sexton, Anne, *Love Poems*
Shakespeare, William, *Hamlet*
Slater, P., *Pursuit of Loneliness*
Smith, Adam, *Powers of Mind*
Sohl, Robert & Can, Audrey (Ed.), *The Gospel According to Zen*
Steinbeck, John, *Of Mice and Men*
Thurber, James, *The Owl in the Attic and Other Perplexities*
Trudeau, G.B., *The President is a Lot Smarter than you Think*
Trudeau, G.B., *Wouldn't a Gremlin Have Been Much More Sensible*
Turkel, Studs (Ed.), *Working*
Viscott, David, M.D. — any of his books
Vonnegut, Kurt, *Breakfast of Champions*
Vonnegut, Kurt, *Cat's Cradle*
Vonnegut, Kurt, *God Bless You, Mr. Rosewater*
Vonnegut, Kurt, *Player Piano*
Vonnegut, Kurt, *Slaughterhouse Five*
Vonnegut, Kurt, *Wampeters, Foma and Granfalloons*
Watts, Alan, *The Book*
Watts, Alan, *The Meaning of Happiness*
Weiner, Jack, *Drinking*
Wheelis, Allen, *The Desert, How People Change, The Moralist*
Williams, Tennessee, *A Streetcar Named Desire*
The Bible
The Koran
The Upanishads
Anything by: E. Albee, J. Baldwin, T.S. Eliot, E. Hemingway, L. Hughes, F. Kafka, D. Lessing, W. Saroyan, J. Sartre, or the St. Mary's Series: *Ritual and Life, Shaping of Self, Search for Meaning, Loneliness*

Music
Popular

Joan Baez, *David's Album*
Beatles, *Abbey Road*
Beatles, *Let It Be*
Beatles, *White Album*
Beatles, *Sgt. Pepper's Lonely Hearts Club Band*
Buffalo Springfield, *Retrospective*
Byrds, *Turn, Turn, Turn*
Harry Chapin, *Verities and Balder Dash*
Harry Chapin, *Heads and Tales*
Harry Chapin, *Sniper and Other Love Songs*
Leonard Cohen, *Songs from the Room*
Leonard Cohen, *Songs of Leonard Cohen*
Judy Collins, *Recollections*
David Crosby, *If I Could Only Remember My Name*
Crosby, Stills, Nash, Young, *Deja Vu*
Bob Dylan, *Highway 61 Revisited*
Bob Dylan, *Freewheelin'*
Bob Dylan, *Another Side of Bob Dylan*
Bob Dylan, *Greatest Hits Vol. I & II*
Fiddler on the Roof
Roberta Flack, *First Take*
Roberta Flack, *Quiet Fire*
Fleetwood Mac, *Rumors*
Richie Havens, *Richard P. Havens, 1983*
Gil Scott Heron, *Pieces of Man*
Gil Scott Heron, *Winter in America*
Incredible String Band, *Changing Horses*
It's a Beautiful Day, *Marrying Maiden*
It's A Beautiful Day, *It's A Beautiful Day*
Jefferson Airplane, *Surrealistic Pillow*
Elton John, *Elton John*
Elton John, *Goodbye Yellow Brick Road*
Elton John, *Friends*
Carole King, anything, especially *Tapestry*
Kris Kristofferson, anything
John Lennon, *Plastic Ono Band*
John Lennon, *Imagine*
Melanie, any selection
Melissa Manchester, *Better Days and Happy Endings*
Melissa Manchester, *Help Is on the Way*
Don McLean, anything
Joni Mitchell, *Ladies of the Canyon*
Joni Mitchell, *Miles of Aisles*
Joni Mitchell, *Clouds*
Maria Muldaur, any selection
Randy Newman, *Good Old Boys*
Randy Newman, *Sail Away*
Tom Paxton, any album
Peter, Paul and Mary, *In the Wind*
Dory Previn, any album
Linda Ronstadt, *Heart Like a Wheel*
Neil Sedaka, any selection
Paul Simon, *Still Crazy After All These Years*
Paul Simon, *Live Rhymin*
Simon and Garfunkel, *Bridge Over Troubled Waters*
Simon and Garfunkel, *Sounds of Silence*

Phoebe Snow, any selection
Cat Stevens, *Teaser and the Firecat*
Cat Stevens, *Tea for the Tillerman*
James Taylor, *Sweet Baby James*
Marlo Thomas, *Free To Be*
The Who, *Tommy*
Stevie Wonder, *Innervisions*
Yes, *The Yes Album*

Jazz

Marion Brown, *Vista*
Alice Coltrane, *Reflection on Creation and Space*
John Coltrane, *A Love Supreme*
John Coltrane, *Transitions*
John Coltrane, *Live in Seattle*
Ahmad Jamal, *Free Flight*
Les McCann, *Invitation to Openness*
Les McCann & Eddie Horn, *Swiss Movement*
Charlie Mingus, *Better Git It In Your Soul*
Wes Montgomery, *A Day in the Life*
Horace Silver Quartet, *That Healin Feelin*
Horace Silver Quartet, *All Horace Silver*
Horace Silver Quartet, *Total Response*
Nina Simone, *Here Comes the Sun*
Nina Simone, *Black Gold*
Nina Simone, *Emergency Ward*

Country and Western

Almost any country and western album is useful in that they capture
attitudes and emotions connected with poverty, sex, broken romances,
booze, rich vs. poor, death.

Comedy

Woody Allen, Bill Cosby, Lenny Bruce, George Carlin

Show Tunes

Man of LaMancha, Joy, Hair, Godspell, West Side Story, Jacques Brel,
Jesus Christ Superstar

Movies

Americanization of Emily
Annie Hall
Bergman's Films — Scenes from A Marriage
                   Face to Face
                   Cries and Whispers

Clockwork Orange	Midnight Cowboy
Days of Wine and Roses	On the Waterfront
The Graduate	Rocky
The Hospital	View from the Bridge
I Never Sang for My Father	West Side Story
The Last Picture Show	A Woman Under the Influence
La Strada	1984
Man in the Wilderness	2001 — A Space Odyssey
Man of La Mancha	

About the Author

Several years ago Lee Silverstein was in his words, "a morally and spiritually bankrupt Peter Pan, seeking only pleasure, loving no one, and committed to nothing."

Since then he has "successfully rechanneled the energy and intensity with which I led a deviant life into a positive force . . . converting the same marketing skills with which I so successfully sold material goods into an ability to influence change in people's lives, thereby bringing them greater satisfaction."

Silverstein has shared those skills in *Consider the Alternative*.

Lee (formerly Director of Human Services at Rockville General Hospital, Rockville, Connecticut) is known nationally for his workshops based on the ideas in the book. If you would like information on any of these ideas, would like him to conduct a workshop in your area, or have some comments on the book, please let him hear from you. Write him at CompCare Publications, 2415 Annapolis Lane, Minneapolis, Minnesota 55441.

Cover design by Aldo Abelleira.
Book design by Jane Eschweiler.

Linda Roberts

Linda Roberts, M.Ed., is a certified school psychologist. Lee Silverstein says about her: "She has the capacity to greet the world with childlike wonder and yet to understand with a mature penetration and to help with enthusiastic resourcefulness."

Jon Brett

Jon Brett currently does counseling for an inpatient alcohol treatment unit at the University of Connecticut Health Center. He received his Master's Degree in psychology from the New York School for Social Research in New York City and has been active for several years in various types of task-oriented group work.

The future
of man
is "to be",
not
"to have".

publications

A Division of the Comprehensive Care Corporation
Post Office Box 27777, Minneapolis, Minnesota 55427

for faster service on charge orders
call us toll free at:

800/328-3330

In Minnesota, call collect 612/559-4800

ORDER FORM

Date _____

| Order Number | Customer Number | Customer P.O. | ☐ 0 | ☐ 1 | ☐ 2 | ☐ 3 | ☐ 4 | **For Office Use Only** |

| UPS 1 ☐ | PP 2 ☐ | PPD 3 ☐ | PPD CHGS 4 ☐ | WILL CALL 5 ☐ | OUR TRUCK 6 ☐ | CARRIER _____ |

BILL ORDER TO:

Name _____

Address _____

City/State/Zip _____

Non-profit organization, please show tax exemption number [   ]

Signature _____ Sales and use tax number _____

SHIP ORDER TO: (If other than above)

Name _____

Address _____

City/State/Zip _____

Telephone _____ Purchase Order (if required) _____

☐ Please send me the CompCare Catalog of more books and
materials for growth-centered living.

Please send me _____ copies of *Consider the Alternative* at $5.95 each.

PLEASE FILL IN BELOW FOR CHARGE ORDERS
Or enclose check for total amount of order.

Prices subject to change without notice.

Account No. (12 or more digits) from your credit card.

| | | | | | | | | | | | |

Check one:
☐ VISA   ☐ MASTER CHARGE   Master Charge—also enter 4 digits below your account no

Your Card Issuing Bank _____

Expiration Date of Card _____

Credit Card Signature _____

TOTAL PRICE _____

4% Sales Tax _____
(Minnesota residents only)

Postage & Handling charge _____
Add 75 cents to orders totaling less than $15.00
Add 5% to orders totaling $15.00 or more.

GRAND TOTAL _____

All orders shipped outside continental
U.S.A. will be billed actual shipping costs.

VISA*   **master charge** THE INTERBANK CARD